PRAISE FOR

BECOMING AN
INDIGO WOMAN

Much like the IndigoWomen Group Coaching Experience, Shayna's book inspires us to introspect while challenging us to believe boldly. I'm truly empowered to live and lead in an awakened state that does not leave me depleted, and Shayna equips us all with the tools and mindset to carry on. Shayna's words prompt us to transform into our most bold and unapologetic selves, and I am truly grateful for her voice!

—**Ashli Wilson**, Academic Specialist, DC Prep

Becoming an IndigoWoman is the guidebook that every woman who is claiming their righteous place in this world should read. With doable and profound guidance, this book will change the way you think about your role—not only in your life but in the lives that you touch, teach, lead, and love. As a Black woman living in this era, this is a book that will help you get started or continue on your journey to thriving.

—**Doris Dupuy**, Administration and Finance Director, Resonance Network

Shayna invites us to "tell the truth" to our community, our loved ones, and, most importantly, to ourselves. This simple (albeit challenging at times) yet profound step is key to transforming how we lead, love, and live our most authentic and fulfilling lives. May Spirit continue to whisper in all our endeavors and crossroads, "Tell the truth."

—**Jennifer Toles**, National Organizer, Black Organizing for Leadership & Dignity

Reading this book is like standing at the mouth of a dark cave and challenging yourself to face your greatest fear: a grounded, better, and more beautiful you. Each chapter resonates more deeply than the last. Each chapter asks you to go deeper within yourself to face things that hold you back from being your fullest, most genuine self. Thank you, Shayna Renee, for being so honest and vulnerable and for opening the space for Black women to stand next to you in the ultimate journey of realizing one's most authentic power source: self! As a member of the inaugural Indigo tribe, I would join you over and over again.

—Kristina Kyles-Smith, Executive Director,
Two Rivers Public Charter School

Shayna Renee is truly depositing seeds of healing not only to take root but for women to have a painfully beautiful birthing into our healing. Shayna's process is truly creating bridges to healing that can be embraced, embodied, and experienced in such a way that women are walking into their full joyfidence. The only "R" missing from this work is Remarkable. Thank you, Shayna, for helping me to witness myself in my rebirth through such powerful work and the words that you speak so powerfully in your writing. They truly watered my soul.

—Marcia Dinkins, Executive Director,
Black Women Rising

FINALLY, FINALLY, FINALLY, a book that puts a name to what Black women have been enduring for centuries but also offers an authentic process on rebirthing our authentic self. Thank you!

—Rachel Briggs, Director of Curriculum and
Administration, Shining Stars Montessori Academy

"Energy is low . . . nurturing relationships that aren't aligned to who we presently are . . ." Whew. I was already a fan of Shayna and her R3 framework. Not only do these strategies speak to my spirit, but also they are actionable—they really helped me to feel like I have true power over myself. After reading this book, I feel enriched. Shayna gives us honesty and helps Black femme folx thrive. So grateful to her—this book is life-changing.

—**Maya Stewart**, Middle School Principal,
DC International School

Becoming an IndigoWoman: How to Thrive in Leadership and Life is filled with questions that prompt you to reflect upon and explore yourself and the life you want to live. The chapter on self-care is a beautiful reminder to care for yourself expansively and to be compassionate with yourself as the first step.

—**Monique Wright**, Senior Director, Leading Educators

As women with many responsibilities, we go through many stages of life. *Becoming an IndigoWoman* is a transformative book that you won't want to put down. Be sure that as you read, you have a journal, pen, highlighter, and open heart. This book takes you through the process of transformation, likened to the butterfly—from the egg to the adult butterfly that's beautiful and free. *Becoming an IndigoWoman* is the roadmap for a woman leader finding her place of oasis, finding her voice, finding herself. Three words sum up this book: RELEASE, HEALING, FREEDOM! Get ready to go on a life-changing and freeing journey with Shayna as you walk in your destiny!

—**Nicole Johnson-Douglas**, Founder and Principal Consultant
at D'vine Touch Education and Management Consulting

As I read *Becoming an IndigoWoman: How to Thrive in Leadership and Life*, I could clearly feel Shayna Renee's voice. Her coaching presence—warm, supportive, and gently uncovering opportunities for growth—comes through as she walks you through her three-phase process to becoming a woman who prioritizes her own self-care because she knows this will also benefit those around her. If you're not able to take part in the IndigoWomen community directly, then I encourage you to use this book to read and work through with a group of sister-friends. Make time to really see and love up on each other as you make a plan for healing and radical self-care.

—**Rachel Kimboko**, Executive Director, DC Wildflower Schools

Published by Mandala Tree Press
www.mandalatreepress.com

Paperback ISBN: 9781954801158
Case Laminate Hardcover ISBN: 9781954801356
Hardcover with Dust Jacket ISBN: 9781954801165
eBook ISBN: 9781954801172

SEL027000 SELF-HELP / Personal Growth / Success
BUS109000 BUSINESS & ECONOMICS / Women in Business
OCC019000 BODY, MIND & SPIRIT / Inspiration & Personal Growth

Cover design by Lisa Barbee
Edited by Valene Wood
Typeset by Kaitlin Barwick

www.indigowomencommunity.com
www.shaynarenee.com

I'd like to dedicate this book to my inner child who didn't always know or understand her worth . . . and yet kept going. Her unmet needs and desires fueled the vision for the *IndigoWomen* community, this book, and the subsequent ripple effects of love and liberation. May everyone's inner child light up with joy, clarity, and conviction as they read the pages ahead.

Contents

Introduction 1

PART I: REBIRTH 11

Chapter 1: (Re)Discover Your Purpose ... 15

Chapter 2: Integrate Self-care
as a Mindset 32

Chapter 3: Tell the Truth 59

PART II: RESET 72

Chapter 4: Lead from the Center 76

Chapter 5: Eliminate Control, Attachments,
and Assumptions 94

Contents

Chapter 6: Trust and Forgive Yourself
            and Others 108

PART III: RENEW 127

Chapter 7: Protect Your Vibe and
            Nurture Your Tribe 130

Chapter 8: Intentionally Love
            Yourself 147

Before I Let Go 160

Acknowledgments 168

About the Author 171

Introduction

SINCE BEING FORCED INTO THIS COUNTRY, SOCIETY has asked Black women to do it all—care for families, hunt for families, harvest for families, lift and till for families, and build entire communities and economies. Flash forward and we are the hardest working women and yet the lowest paid. We start companies at higher rates than any other cultural group, set cultural and global trends, and are the backbones of our families, prayer warriors who conjure the impossible, and healers who see what most can't. We are magnificence personified—and yet, and yet, and yet.

The time has come for Black women to convene, heal, and rise. No one can see us like we can; no one can hear us like we can. Generations of compounded pain have gone unaddressed, unacknowledged, or unknown. But there's an opening; there's a critical mass of us—I call us *IndigoWomen*—who feel and are breaking the generational wounds that have plagued our families for so long. We understand that when we heal, we heal several generations forward and backward. We understand it's through our own transformations that the other Black women in our spheres will be called higher. Simplified, *IndigoWomen* are free Black women. This isn't about evangelizing; it isn't about a sermon. This is about the mundane, repetitive decisions to turn inward for wisdom and outward for service.

Becoming an IndigoWoman: How to Thrive in Leadership and Life is for those who hear the call that says, "It's time to rise. It's time to delve deeper into a spiritual journey of self-discovery. It's time to turn toward fear and run through it." We know on the other side of fear is the road map to our greatest desires and calling. Yes, abundance is our birthright. We are entitled to the absolute best life offers.

You may be thinking, "I feel that, but what's up with the name *IndigoWoman*?" A few years ago, when I was stuck in a pattern of shrinking and hiding my voice, my therapist asked me to come up with a word that would immediately remind me of my divine power. My first thought was that the word needed to combine both the masculine and feminine energies within me. I took a deep breath and the word *indigo* surfaced right away. My feet tingled, my shoulders dropped, and I felt a sense of aliveness that was both familiar and powerfully new at

NOTES

the same time. The color indigo is a blend of two primary colors that many associate with the masculine and feminine—blue and red, resulting in a mixture between blue and violet. The cool blue attributes of indigo symbolize trust, stability, communication, meditation, and peace, while the violet attributes of indigo symbolize royalty, spiritual wisdom, higher self, justice, and fairness. I called upon these attributes as I elevated as a leader and navigated through my spiritual awakening and growth journey. So did many other Black women—cis, trans, and nonbinary—I had the honor of coaching, leading, knowing, and being in community with.

As *IndigoWomen*, we see through the illusions of margins, systemic racism, patriarchy, and oppression. We know we didn't create those constructs, and they are manifestations of someone else's spiritual illness. That illness has manifested as the sick collective consciousness that has plagued every colonized country in our world. Yes, America is deeply infected. It is infected with white supremacy and some of its worst symptoms show up as patriarchy, sexism, homophobia, xenophobia, and several other isms that purport one group is superior or more deserving than another. We all, regardless of our racial, cultural, or gender expression, are steeped in systems, institutions, and environments ravaged with this infection, and we all have the capacity and choice to get and remain well. Like with any illness, we must first be aware that we are ill, then we must commit to a treatment plan, and finally we must make necessary lifestyle adjustments in order to remain well.

IndigoWomen are aware, and continually gaining a deeper awareness, of the ways they've been infected with the sick collective consciousness. We know and embody what Audre Lorde said long ago:

> "The true focus of revolutionary change is never merely the oppressive situations that we seek to escape, but that piece of the oppressor which is planted deep within each of us."[1]

We understand that our racial reckoning work is simple—to heal and remain on a healing path. That beautiful, healing path can be experienced as a freedom to thrive, to live life expecting and commanding abundance and liberation.

---

1. Lorde, Audre. *Sister Outsider: Essays and Speeches* (United Kingdom: Crossing Press, 1984).

NOTES

You may wonder, "Are we the only ones called to heal and remain on a healing path?" Of course not. There are white people and other people of color who know this truth and are consciously doing their work of self-discovery. They know the construct of whiteness isn't who they are, and they are making progress, disrupting inequities, and calling others higher in their unique ways. That critical mass is growing. And as an aside, if you represent that critical mass, you are welcome to join and grow with us in the pages ahead as coconspirators and people who love the Black women in their spheres. Just keep in mind, when I say "we," I'm speaking to all Black woman-identified and feminine people and our experiences. Too often, our needs and reality get sidetracked because others call upon us to support them in their work. They want us to justify and legitimize their growth and labor and expect us to be the mammies of humanity. Not today.

Black women, from Harriet Tubman and Fannie Lou Hamer to Maya Angelou and Audre Lorde, have always been the leaders of humanity. Moving forward, today and every day, it's time for us to boldly operate as such. Black women, when grounded, can hold multiple truths, paths, solutions, and emotions all while caring for our families, tribes, and communities. We also tell the truth. We understand what dear Maya Angelou said a long time ago: "There's a world of difference between truth and facts. Facts can obscure the truth." We can size up a room, a person, and a situation in seconds. We're swift, to the point, and miles ahead of everyone in the room. We have radars for virtually everything—predators, liars, overseers, manipulators, and also geniuses, visionaries, underdogs, and revolutionaries.

Versatile doesn't even come close to describing our power because it doesn't capture the vertical depth we have. We know the pain of neglect and the joy of genius personified. We encapsulate the possibility of love, redemption, and the eradication of centuries of oppression. We are both the test and the answer. As a deeply marginalized and mistreated community, America's wellness and moral compass can be measured by how well it cares for us, while at the same time, looks to us for the remedy. Why do you think folks always hire a Black woman when shit hits the fan? We were the ones cautioning misguided decisions from the very beginning. We were shaking our heads while our perspectives were shaken back to the margins time and time again. We've played every position on every team. We know the plays,

NOTES

we wrote the strategy, and we've studied the competition on both sides. We've had to in order to survive.

Black women have always been on our own team, and today, as the world checks into the Intensive Care Unit, we are checking ourselves into community with one another. We are forming our own cocoons of healing, self-discovery, and joy. Black women know all too well what many are just now noticing about the illness of our world. Our cells know it; our ancestors knew it, and now our ancestors are calling on us to rise, to thrive. We must recommit each day to tell the truth to ourselves about ourselves. We have to dare to be courageous enough to ask: "What's mine to own and what do I need to release?"

WHAT'S MINE TO OWN AND WHAT DO I NEED TO RELEASE?

Some of us are so great at adjusting other people's crowns we get caught in cycles of slipping back into sleepwalking mode. Our pain can usurp our minds and make us believe pain is who we are. In this state, we can take on a victim mentality:

- We think life is happening to us and not for us.
- We believe everyone is out to get us.

- We settle for the same kinds of toxic and dysfunctional relationships we were born into.
- We believe we can't have more because we don't see more in our immediate environment.
- We believe we are our circumstances.
- We believe we are the margins.

Black women are and always have been right in the center—the epicenter of humanity. This isn't fleeting poetry or moving rhetoric; I channel this through Spirit, right back to you, now. Fight the feeling and old paradigm thinking that says, "This feels like we're inserting ourselves as superior to others. Aren't we creating the same consciousness that got us here?" No, hear and feel me. We are neither better than, superior to, or any more deserving of liberation than anyone else. We are just uniquely positioned in this lifetime to empathize with what it means to get marginalized, and to know and embody the kinds of leadership that will shepherd us into a fresh way of being, living, working, and leading. This is why I often say: When Black women thrive, humanity thrives.

WHEN BLACK WOMEN THRIVE, HUMANITY THRIVES.

NOTES

Black women are no longer waiting for some pro-
lific person, group, or movement to challenge us to rise.
Instead, what I offer and channel here is a method, the
R3 Method™, to heal and transform our minds, bodies,
and spirits so that we may thrive while leading boldly.
Many of us have heard this call in the deep recesses of
our spirits. We've heard it in our meditations and seen
visions and dreams of what a new world looks and feels
like. Know you're not alone; you're not crazy; you're not
arrogant; and you're certainly not birthing the same consciousness that got us into our current reality. You are
likely tired, frustrated, and stretched too thin. Light a
candle, curl up with your favorite beverage, have a journal and pen handy, and take this journey of rebirthing,
resetting, and renewing your mind, body, and soul.

This book is organized into the three parts of the R3
Method™—Rebirth, Reset, and Renew—hence R cubed.
There are spiritually inspired and research-based frame-
works, stories, perspectives, and practices woven into
each part that may serve you better and have already supported the elevation and transformation of Black woman
leaders within various sectors across the country. Be
open, be courageous, and take these words back to your

ancestors and ask for guidance on how you're to integrate and/or reteach them. Let's get it.

Part I

REBIRTH

S – Set the Vision through Your Purpose(s)
I – Integrate Self-Care as a Mindset
T – Tell the Truth

SIT STILL.

THIS FIRST PART OF THE R3 METHOD™, REBIRTH, represents an intention to evaluate and experience who we really are and what we're uniquely positioned to do in order to embody the love and authentic leadership style necessary for our life's purpose. Discovering and declaring *who* we are and *what* we're uniquely positioned to do can seem daunting given various competing priorities, our fast-paced lives, packed calendars, the needs of loved ones, and the implications the answers could have on everyone within our spheres. Oftentimes we don't realize that our energy is low not just due to physical exhaustion, but because we're spending most of our waking hours performing tasks and nurturing relationships that aren't aligned with who we presently are and what we're calling in. After fifteen years of coaching executive and director-level leaders, I've learned that once women begin carving out time to prioritize and care for themselves, they become more aware of what they need and want—unlocking their capacity to dream about and manifest a more authentic leadership style.

Most of us know, on some level, that we have to put our own oxygen mask on first so that we can give and lead from a full cup, but in the beginning of this process, my clients often ask questions and make statements like these:

- How do I not feel guilty about centering self-care when I'm the only one in my household or organization who does?

- How do I make peace with the ways in which I've betrayed or dishonored myself?

- How do I center self-care while continuing to elevate, take on more responsibility

⟶ NOTES ⟶

at work, prioritize my love partnership, and raise children?

- How do I convince myself, team, manager/board that self-care work is important enough to prioritize right now?

- I start off great and then get sucked into working on weekends, after hours, etc. How do I stick to a self-care regimen?

- I love what I do, but I feel completely depleted and exhausted by the time the day ends. How do I create the energy and time to meditate or spend time with myself?

- My health is deteriorating and I don't know where to begin.

- I tend to only do this kind of work when I burnout, have a health issue, or a particular mini crisis at work. How do I know when it's time to reprioritize how I spend my time and center self-care?

Which questions resonate with you? What new questions emerged? Jot them down and set an intention for what you'd like to learn, experience, and manifest after reading the Rebirth process.

NOTES

Chapter 1

(RE)DISCOVER YOUR PURPOSE

THE FIRST WHISPER CAME WHILE I WAS IN college: "You're here to teach." It was profoundly clear and yet far from what I was currently studying. However, it wasn't far at all from my love of children. I interpreted that message literally as, "You're to teach children in schools," and that's what I did.

My first day of teaching third grade was among my best days. I'd already met with every parent of each child prior to the first day. I knew their goals for their children. I even knew how to best configure the seating. I called our classroom the Home of the High-Achievers. At the very beginning, I made it clear we weren't just there to learn third-grade content. We were there to excel, build community, and believe in a power greater than all of us.

We began each morning with goal setting and a class mantra. We created community agreements around what it meant to be a High-Achiever and believed that was exactly who we were, and we expected the absolute best from ourselves and each other. I was clear from the beginning that I was teaching them the power of belief, love, and reverence for self and each other. Two years later, after I won a coveted teaching award for having the highest academic gains, I was told it wasn't just because some students jumped four whole grade levels in reading and math in just one year with me, it was because I cultivated a community that connected students to what life is truly about outside the classroom. I honored the responsibility I had to create a safe, nurturing, and high-vibrating community. We had our own chants, rituals, routines, and even dances to keep the energy high, joy filled, rigorous, and loving.

As the years went on, though, Spirit completed Her sentence: "You're here to teach the masses." *Holy shit. What does that mean?* The "masses" part intimidated me—and still does when I don't center myself. Because of my early success in the classroom and the external growth of charter schools in our state and country, my career ushered me into school leadership at the ripe age of twenty-five. No longer teaching third-graders, I was now training and leading people who were more than twice my age. I thought this might be what Spirit meant by teaching the masses. I was the second youngest person on staff. Yet, I was the bridge between the founding team of teachers

NOTES

and the new teachers. My childhood years of leading sports teams groomed me to understand and know my natural leadership instincts. The pressure was thick, the jealousy was in the smog, and the anticipation of what my leadership would mean echoed throughout the walls of the entire school. I made plenty of mistakes, lost some dear edu-friends through the shift in power dynamics, and also translated classroom success into a middle school that became the highest-performing in Baltimore.

I'm often asked what was the greatest lesson I learned there and what gift did the teachers, staff, and families give me. Truthfully, they taught me the single most important leadership skill: listening. While I was a skilled listener of my students, I learned on the job how to listen to and synthesize multiple adult perspectives and then translate what I was hearing into practices, policies, systems, and experiences. I knew school was much more than a place to learn; it's a place to experience life. For me, school was both my refuge and a place where I felt the painful impacts of racism. At a young age, I balanced multiple truths: enduring various forms of abuse at home; being implicitly and explicitly taught at school that I wasn't as smart as the white children; and while I felt inferior for many of my school years, I still cherish some fond memories of fun school events and a catalytic fifth-grade teacher who was the first person in my life to acknowledge my brilliance and budding leadership skills. As a school leader, I determined that our students, our classrooms, and our school, would be identity affirming, joy filled, rigorous, liberating, and loving. I'd like to think that was what I was teaching the adults, too—it is not only possible to have fun while performing at the highest levels, but a necessity.

Eventually, after a few reflective years post school leadership, it hit me. *That's it!* I'm here to teach people how to live in such a way that they experience joy while channeling their power, exuding radiance, being authentic, and embodying love—all these things work together to create a ripple effect of liberation. We are all meant to thrive. However, we have currently made global agreements that some thrive at the expense of others. We've agreed you take what you want and do whatever it takes to keep what you have. We're at a reckoning—karmic debts are owed. Scarcity's time is up. White supremacy's time is up. Patriarchy's time is up. The divine feminine is rising. Those once pushed to the margins are now in the center.

NOTES

Throughout my spiritual growth journey, I've learned that (re)discovering your life's purpose is about being present to what Spirit, or whatever you call your higher power, is calling you to hear while also paying present attention to the patterns unfolding in your life. As we grow and evolve, our life's purpose grows, expands, and changes with us. One practice to support this level of self-discovery is to ask Spirit for one spiritual principle to focus upon each year. Then turn that principle into an intention. For example, when I first started doing this practice many years ago, my first spiritual principle was courage. The intention for that year was "to be courageous for the purpose of rediscovering myself and my life's purpose." What I didn't know then that I understand now is when you set an intention for something, its opposite will show up in your life to give you opportunities to practice and embody that principle. *Shit.*

I was in for a year of life presenting me with situations, circumstances, and people that scared the shit out of me. It was that year when I had to tell the truth to myself about how unhappy I was in my marriage; the impact it was going to have on my children terrified me. We've all read and heard about the negative effects divorce can have on children, and that's where my worried thoughts flowed. And yet, my intention was to "be courageous."

I went back to therapy, both individual and marriage counseling. I told the truth and deepened my self-awareness, and I gained the strength to set myself free from that marriage. While that was the major circumstance in my life at the time, it certainly wasn't the only one. There were other moments of awareness about how to use my voice, other ways I had betrayed myself and given my power away. That was one of the most transformative years of my life. I discovered the most courageous thing I could do in life, that we can all do in our lives, is to tell the truth.

First, we must tell the truth to ourselves about ourselves and then tell the truth to the people in our communities. In a world where some of us are more open on social media than we are in front of humans, it's important to emphasize the significance of the energetic exchange that happens when two humans decide to open up and reveal a piece of themselves. There's a force field of love, trust, and connectedness that happens between the individuals agreeing to see and honor what's being shared. This kind of mutual agreement doesn't happen on social media. Social media is one-way

NOTES

communication. We decide and curate what we share with no agreement on the other end around how, when, or whether it will get received. Tell the truth to yourself. Tell the truth to those in your community who have earned the right to hear your truth. Learn from and embody it and then decide how you'd like to share it beyond that.

The first step is to stop where you are, right now, and ask yourself what spiritual principle you are being called to learn and embody. Trust what comes to you right away, no matter what your mind says about it. Turn that principle into an intention that focuses on how you want to show up in the world and for the people who matter to you most. Write it down and prepare to be open to life's lessons, gifts, and miracles.

It's important to listen not just to what people say but also to what life is saying, what your place of work is saying, and what your results are saying.

IT'S IMPORTANT TO LISTEN NOT JUST TO WHAT PEOPLE SAY BUT ALSO TO WHAT LIFE IS SAYING, WHAT YOUR PLACE OF WORK IS SAYING, AND WHAT YOUR RESULTS ARE SAYING.

- What is the message?

- What is the common thread?

- What are people and conflicts saying about you?

When I noticed this trend, I created what's called the "JCC." Before an *IndigoWoman* envisions a fresh way of living or leading, she needs to know her JCC—her Jam, her Craft, and her Calling. Our Jam is that gift or talent which brings us absolute joy. It's that thing we would do for free and for hours on end; we lose track of time when we're exercising it.

In the book *The Big Leap*, Gay Hendricks talks about how we live in certain zones.[2] We exercise our Jam when we are in the Genius Zone. When we're operating in this zone, we are in a state of flow where our intuition guides our next steps. We don't have to think too much about what we're doing because we're having fun and effortlessly making a positive impact on ourselves and those around us. I included a positive impact on ourselves because some of us cocreate amazing impacts for others, but it exhausts or depletes us. If that is the case, whatever came to mind might not be your Jam.

2. Hendricks, Gay, *The Big Leap: Conquer Your Hidden Fear and Take Life to the Next Level* (United States: HarperOne, 2009).

For me, it is coaching. Fewer things bring me more joy than seeing others light up and literally walk, talk, and live with more conviction, love, and light. I love the feeling of not knowing the questions I will ask and trusting my intuition to reveal the divine right next question that resonates with my client and her context. Watching my clients deepen their self-awareness and rediscover parts of themselves is exhilarating. To me, coaching is a dance. Each client brings a new rhythm, melody, and hook. I partner with them to dance and flow through their various fears, desires, awareness, and commitments and through it all, magic happens. Rather than making a particular outcome happen, I channel inspiration from Spirit.

I've always shown up like a coach throughout my life. I'm naturally curious about people—what motivates, terrifies, excites, and disgusts them. When other small children were asking themselves what toy they wanted to play with next, I was asking myself, "Is this what life is all about?" Why people do what they do and how they could change their lives has always fascinated me. I've always been the "strong friend," the rock, the one people share things with that they wouldn't share with anyone else. Much like in my first classroom as a teacher, I intuitively know how to create safe containers for exponential learning and growth. It brings me immense joy.

I'm grateful I could translate some of what I learned as a teacher into my coaching method and approach. Some people don't have a Jam close to what they are trained to do. Others of us can get so praised for what we're traditionally trained to do that we confuse that thing for our Jam when it's really our Craft. Our Craft is that gift or talent we've learned or honed over a long period. It could be a vocation you went to school for or the thing you do for a living. You like it and take delight in having an impact, but it doesn't necessarily bring you the joy your Jam does.

Many of my former clients discovered they're exhausted or bored in their jobs because they confused their Craft with their Jam and didn't know to envision something grander for themselves. According to Hendrick's zones, we exercise our Craft in the Competence Zone. In this zone, we apply our studies and lessons learned to create some sort of set of outcomes. This may be the thing you secretly don't like, but are nervous to admit to yourself or others, because you fear what it means for how you make a living or relate to the people currently in your life. If this applies to you,

NOTES

breathe. It doesn't mean you need to abandon whatever it is; it just might mean you need to apply this awareness to how you express your Craft. For example, my Jam is coaching, but my Craft is teaching. I became a third-grade teacher right out of college and earned my first master's degree in the art of teaching. I enjoy taking complex concepts and breaking them down into digestible pieces. I love creating the environment necessary for meaningful learning to happen. I have a knack for planning but yearn for less structure at the same time. I'm also not crazy about the grading and assessment pieces of teaching, and the medium can sometimes feel too limiting and distant for me in terms of the depth I can go to with others.

To make teaching more enjoyable for me, I applied (and still apply), a coaching stance to it and act more like a facilitator than the sage on the stage. I make sure my students do the heavy lifting, do most of the talking, and have room to make and learn from mistakes. I'm well known for my ability to teach and facilitate groups of any size, both virtually and in person. What everyone may not realize is that it's my coaching stance that makes my facilitation have such a transformative impact. I intentionally infuse my Jam into my Craft, and that's where the magic happens. Even as I write this first book, in order to bring it to fruition, I've had to adjust my mindset around the process and flow and treat it like a coaching engagement. I take delight in including powerful questions, stretch activities, conscious sharing, and invitations to envision a grander version of you. I told myself everyone who picked up this book chose me as their coach, and we're in a dance. Now it doesn't hurt that my Jam and Craft are like creative cousins in that they are related and under the same umbrella.

One of my former clients discovered her Jam was creating art like drawings, paintings, and pottery. Her Craft was selling insurance. She excelled quickly in her company and took delight in teaching her direct reports to sell effectively. When I asked her how she taught others, she mentioned she'd have her direct reports draw or find images that inspired them to describe the purpose and benefits of insurance. She did it instinctively and didn't realize that she was infusing her Jam to make her Craft more fun to do. With this new awareness, she more intentionally and frequently infused art into how she led and managed, meaning she gets to experience much more joy day-to-day while also continuing to excel. She didn't have to quit her career in insurance to pursue one

NOTES

in art—unless she really wanted to. Often, we just need to tweak the intentionality behind how we lead and live.

Speaking of how we lead and live, some of us need or want clarity around what we're here to do. This is what we call our Calling. Our Calling is that thing or set of things we feel energetically compelled to do. It represents a theme or pattern we see pop up in our lives repeatedly. For example, a pattern in my life that keeps surfacing over and over is the opportunity to lead. Even when I try to set the intention to sit back and be observant, a challenge will surface, and I'm usually called to lead more deliberately in some way. This pattern surfaces in both my personal and professional life.

Our calling is sometimes that thing that also scares us. For many years, I feared certain aspects of leadership, especially the aspects that invited me to be seen, heard, or valued in grand and public ways. I shied away from speaking engagements, refused to engage on social media, and didn't spend the time necessary on growing my businesses to reach more people. Still today, I lean on my own coach and therapist to make sure I'm not subconsciously succumbing to the fear of my Calling to lead. And most importantly, I've learned to trust my own way of leading which is cocreating safe containers and environments where people can step into the best versions of themselves.

Some clients ask me whether I believe we all have one purpose or many purposes. I've come to understand it's different for everyone. For me, I have four purposes; however, I've coached several clients who have one purpose, and others who have experienced various levels of the same purpose unfolding in different ways in their lives. Callings aren't revealed on an intellectual level; they are simply felt emotionally and spiritually. The best way to tap into your Calling is to become a nonjudgmental observer of your life. Ask yourself the following questions, then journal about the answers and see what emerges.

THE BEST WAY TO TAP INTO YOUR CALLING IS TO BECOME A NONJUDGMENTAL OBSERVER OF YOUR LIFE.

- What events in my life were challenging, and what role did I play in those events?

- What do others often rely on me for?

- What way of being scares me, yet I feel compelled to embody over and over?

NOTES

Once we know our JCC, we're able to birth a grander way of being, living, and leading for ourselves. Knowing our JCC is the first step toward adopting self-care as a mindset. Often, we exhaust ourselves because we don't have an awareness of what our JCC is, and we've gotten stuck into an autopilot mode of living and leading. We're doing what we think others expect of us or what we're obligated to do and not what brings us joy. No amount of rest, baths, or spa days will fill the void of not operating in our JCC. Caring for and putting ourselves first begins with knowing who we are and why we're here.

To anchor the JCC in what the next career or personal endeavor may be, I guide clients to draw four circles. They designate three of them for their Jam, Craft, and Calling and the fourth for the answers to the following two questions:

- What kind of life do you want to live?

- What would you do and experience if fear weren't an option?

The answers can include how they want to feel, how they'd like to spend their time, who they'd like to spend it with, what kind of environment they'd like to live in, what kind of car they'd like to drive, what they want for the people in the core of their lives (i.e. family members, partner, or children), what kinds of trips or adventures they'd like to take, and what they'd like to learn. The key is to have fun and be specific while making this list.

After describing what's in the four circles, clients set an intention to discover what job, role, or way of being blends aspects of all four spheres. Many clients have found it supportive to wait a day or two after discovering their JCC to do this part. Inspiration and guidance may arrive through a conversation with a loved one about their JCC or from a complete stranger. They just need to be open to what emerges.

NOTES

NOTES

Chapter 2

INTEGRATE SELF-CARE AS A MINDSET

WHEN AMID MAJOR BREAKDOWN AND TRANSFOR-mation, a spiritual guide once told me, "Shayna, when you learn to put your self-care first, your life will roll out like a red carpet. You will be the star in your life, and everything else will fall into place with ease." I really wanted to believe her, but I didn't have a vision or example for what that looked like at the time. I was preparing for divorce, had just launched my first business Lead For Liberation (formerly known as Teach To Lead), and had two small children who were about to find out their home foundations were broken in half. I was terrified, guilt ridden, and more stressed than I'd been in a long time. What I didn't realize until years later, after much reflection, was that I was also emotionally lonely. I'd been on autopilot for so long, I didn't realize I'd become a stranger to myself. I didn't yet know how to teach people how to treat me or that I even needed to do that. I prioritized my children, my work, and the needs of other loved ones before acknowledging or attending to my own. My fear of how the divorce would affect my children overshadowed my needs.

Thankfully, a good girlfriend suggested acupuncture as a first step. About a year into the practice, while lying on the acupuncture table, I finally told the truth that I was afraid to say to myself and out loud: I felt suffocated within my marriage, and I'd married out of a place of brokenness and misalignment. My marriage was a trauma response. My acupuncturist allowed me to sit in the deafening silence after saying it, and I knew in that moment I had to liberate myself. I didn't know how or when; I just knew major change was on the way.

That's the thing about telling the truth; it has the power to reveal a vision for what the next level-up phase of life looks like. When I told myself the truth about how I truly felt in my marriage and how I got there, I knew I couldn't go back to living on autopilot. I'd created a gap between my state of being before that acupuncture session and after it, and that gap represented a deepened self-awareness about what I was really feeling and why.

What I also realize now that I didn't realize then was that my truth was much bigger than my marriage. My marriage was a symptom of me not yet choosing to live authentically. To live authentically, you must know and live in harmony with the vision and values for your own life.

I had taken no time to truly discover what those were for me. I felt stuck between the awareness of my misalignment and the path toward authenticity.

One of the most important decisions for us to make when we're in the gap between the awareness of misalignment and the path toward authenticity is . . . the decision to be happy. There's a song by Kirk Franklin called "I Smile," which talks about the importance of choosing happiness.[3] After a sad breakup from a post-divorce partner, I played that song repeatedly. I wasn't truly happy in the relationship, and I realized in some of those moments of reflection I hadn't even truly made the deliberate choice to be happy in general, let alone discovered what happiness meant for me.

I'll say that again; I hadn't yet decided to be happy.

---

3. Franklin, Kirk, "I Smile," track 1 on *Hello Fear*, released 22 March 2011 by Verity.

NOTES

It never really occurred to me that happiness is a choice and not just something that haphazardly happens in some people's lives more than others. Happiness is a deliberate decision to prioritize ease over struggle, peace over drama, and simple over convoluted.

HAPPINESS IS A DELIBERATE DECISION TO PRIORITIZE EASE OVER STRUGGLE, PEACE OVER DRAMA, AND SIMPLE OVER CONVOLUTED.

Many books and articles talk about similar aspects of happiness, but what I've yet to hear self-help or leadership gurus talk about are the conditions that more easily allow for such happiness exploration and embodiment. I don't recall happiness ever being discussed in my household, while hard work got discussed quite frequently. As the daughter of two first-generation college graduates, I received clear messages about the significance of having and meeting high expectations, working extremely hard, and being the best. There weren't discussions about how I felt or desired to feel as I was progressing in the schooling process or within athletics. The focus was solely on outcomes.

My experience isn't unique, and it's not unique because Black women have been historically, socially, and politically conditioned to believe our purpose, value, and survival depends on working harder than anyone else while also being supernatural, self-sacrificing caregivers. That conditioning got rooted in the effects of colonization and the expectation for Black women to serve as both subservient Mammies to white families and as hardworking field workers. Society expected us to not only care for, on demand, the family in the Big House, but also expected us to pick cotton, oversee other enslaved Africans, and to do those things graciously, exhibiting no emotion about it.

Flash forward to the present in a society that has yet to reconcile and heal from the pains of our racist past and present. I coach many Black women who realize they unconsciously use work as a distraction to escape from emotions below the surface that they didn't know existed. Instead, they throw themselves into their jobs and into our capitalistic society, and get rewarded for it. Many suppress both positive and undesirable emotions, focusing steadfastly on achieving. Some of them experience emotional loneliness that began in their childhoods and extended into their marriages. What many of them know on subconscious levels, and maybe a bit consciously, is that they're operating inside of a schema that invited them to work unbelievably hard and give

NOTES

in a way that sacrifices their individual needs. Namely, many leaders I coach operate within, have benefitted from, and have become exhausted by the Strong Black Woman Schema.[4]

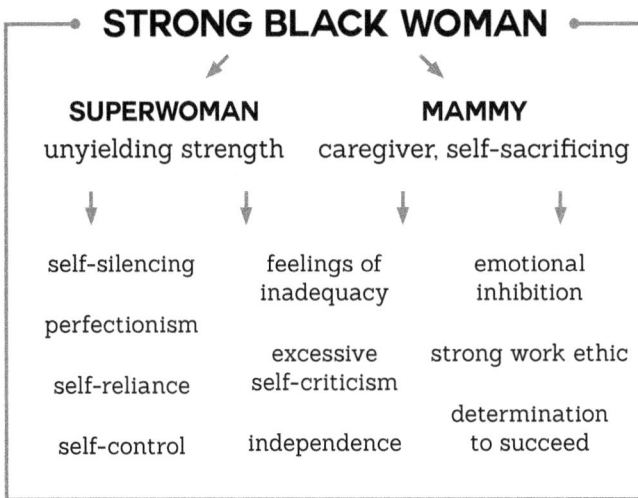

```
┌─────●  STRONG BLACK WOMAN  ●─────┐
│              ↙         ↘              │
│      SUPERWOMAN         MAMMY         │
│   unyielding strength   caregiver, self-sacrificing │
│                                        │
│      ↓        ↓        ↓        ↓      │
│                                        │
│   self-silencing   feelings of      emotional │
│                    inadequacy       inhibition │
│   perfectionism                               │
│                      excessive    strong work ethic │
│   self-reliance    self-criticism             │
│                                   determination │
│   self-control     independence    to succeed │
└────────────────────────────────────────┘
```

4. Liao, Kelly Yu-Hsin, Meifen Wei, and Mengxi Yin. "The Misunderstood Schema of the Strong Black Woman: Exploring Its Mental Health Consequences and Coping Responses Among African American Women." *Psychology of Women Quarterly* 44, no. 1 (March 2020): 84–104. https://doi.org /10.1177/0361684319883198.

Choosing to be happy may sound easy, but when it's not baked into the structural fabric of our country or world, and it was a rarity for one's ancestors, it can seem fleeting, frivolous, radical, and even counterproductive. Many of us have this schema to thank for our professional and financial success. What we may not be asking ourselves is: What did it cost us, and was it worth it?

WHAT DID IT COST US, AND WAS IT WORTH IT? Some clients often ask something like, "Well, if I acknowledge that it cost me happiness in some way, won't I lose the edge in my career I worked so hard to build? I like who I've become and what I've accomplished." When those kinds of wonderings surface, I follow up with questions like:

- What belief needs to expand or be released for you to experience more happiness in your life?

- What support do you need to experience more happiness?

The danger in only answering the first question is that it assumes only the will of the woman needs to shift

NOTES

to invite more happiness. Society supports this schema in every aspect of our environments. The conditions we operate within also need to shift with our raised consciousness. When we decide to operate at an elevated level, we invite everyone within our ecosystem to think about us and themselves in fresh ways. Support might look like setting and communicating boundaries around when and how much we work, delegating tasks that don't align with our JCC, and advocating for or implementing work conditions that allow for everyone to be and give their best. Success and happiness are not mutually exclusive, even though for us, they were intended to be.

For us, closing the gap between the awareness of misalignment and living authentically is generational healing work in the form of integrating self-care as a mindset. When we close this gap, we heal several generations back and all of them moving forward.

When coaching leaders who become aware that they are in the gap and are having a hard time choosing and experiencing happiness, I explain that

FOR US, CLOSING THE GAP BETWEEN THE AWARENESS OF MISALIGNMENT AND LIVING AUTHENTICALLY IS GENERATIONAL HEALING WORK IN THE FORM OF INTEGRATING SELF-CARE AS A MINDSET.

the path through the gap is making self-care personal. There isn't a right or wrong way to do self-care. Caring for our emotional, spiritual, physical, mental, social, financial, and practical well-being requires a commitment to deepen our self-awareness about the source of our stress, exhaustion, or missed opportunities to be and give our best. I invite them to ask themselves questions like, "What is my body telling me?" or "What would bring me joy today?" Answers to these questions vary from person to person and usually involve nurturing the mind, body, and spirit in some way.

Most people have a narrow set of self-care practices they revert to in challenging times. Someone experiencing stress at work may take a warm bath or go for a walk following a tough day. Both are supportive practices because they engage the body. We hold trauma in our bodies, and it's through our physical form that we can efficiently move the trauma out of our bodies. Taking this approach deeper, integrating self-care as a mindset means we weave in and out of practices that support us in both challenging *and* thriving times. A friend recently asked me how much time I spend on self-care each day, and I couldn't answer him. When I'm operating within my JCC, I'm exercising self-care.

NOTES

When I'm choosing to live authentically, I'm exercising self-care. When I'm noticing and deepening my breathing, I'm exercising self-care. When I'm advocating for myself, I'm exercising self-care. What has helped former clients shift from implementing self-care practices only in times of dire need to adopting self-care as a mindset is first expanding what self-care looks like.

SELF-CARE BUCKET EXERCISE

When facilitating the groups of Black woman leaders in the *IndigoWoman Group Coaching Experience*, I invite clients to brainstorm and categorize various self-care practices into the following buckets:

SELF-CARE BUCKETS

emotional | social | physical | financial

mental | spiritual | practical

The women discuss what they do and desire to do to support each aspect of their lives. For example, practices in the emotional bucket would support them in experiencing and releasing targeted emotions, like therapy or writing in a journal. Practices in the social bucket would support them in building or nurturing important relationships in their lives, like setting up virtual happy hours or calling a friend. Practices in the physical bucket would support moving their bodies in some way, like running or stretching, or feeding their bodies high vibration foods, like vegetables or fruit. Practices in the mental bucket would support them in using their brains in different ways, like doing a crossword puzzle or coloring. Practices in the spiritual bucket would support them in connecting with their inner or higher selves, like through prayer or meditation. Practices in the practical bucket would support them in organizing and/or executing tasks that relieve stress in their lives, like hiring a cleaning service or decluttering their desk. Practices in the financial bucket would support them in learning about and managing their money in ways that support their life vision, like creating a budget or partnering with a financial advisor. In the end, they end up with an expanded list of practices and are invited to try

NOTES

one new practice and journal about the impact that it has on them. If doing this activity individually, it's best to spend some time polling a few people within your sphere. Ask them both what they do and desire to do to support their self-care.

Sometimes we use the same set of narrow practices because we simply haven't thought of how else it could look, or we haven't yet deepened our self-awareness to where we know what we need in different contexts. Something I've learned to do is re-engage in therapy when I'm trying something new or embarking on another level-up phase in life. I no longer wait until things have fallen apart.

I NO LONGER WAIT UNTIL THINGS HAVE FALLEN APART.

I know that level-up phases for me often surface alternate versions of age-old fears that formed in childhood. I've noticed this is true for many of my clients as well. It's a good practice to have a flexible self-care plan to support you until it becomes an embodied part of who you are. At the end of each *IndigoWoman* group coaching journey, each woman creates and shares their "Center Self-Care Plan," and I'm always astounded by how creative, expansive, and specific each woman's self-care regimen ends up being.

Clients often ask me whether I think any of the buckets are more important than others, and I always highlight the spiritual bucket. My dear late grandmother, Reverend Eliza Mae Hammond, said, "Because our spirits are what we come into this world with, how others experience us, and the only thing we will leave behind, it should be the first thing that we take care of." *Yup, mic drop.* She spoke in mic drops. She sadly passed away when I was only nine, but undeniably impacted me more than anyone in my life.

My grandmother was love personified. Her mere presence made me and everyone around her sit up a little straighter, be more mindful of our words, and know we were deeply loved. She was a visionary, a leader, a mother of nine, a prophet, and the first woman to become a minister in her church. I grew up hearing stories about folk in the neighborhood lining up to be prayed over by her. She definitely accessed all six of her senses with precision and would likely be called enlightened by many today. To me, she's Grandma, and I still call on her for strength, guidance, and peace. Because she affected me in such a short period, she taught me Maya Angelou's quote cannot be truer:

————— • **NOTES** •———————————————————————•

"I've learned that people will forget what you said, people will forget what you did, but people will never forget how you made them feel."

There's a direct correlation between how we treat people and how we take care of our inner selves. Observe the correlation in your life. Do you notice a difference in how you express yourself, experience your day, treat others, and move through your work when you center yourself before you begin your day?

DO YOU NOTICE A DIFFERENCE IN HOW YOU EXPRESS YOURSELF, EXPERIENCE YOUR DAY, TREAT OTHERS, AND MOVE THROUGH YOUR WORK WHEN YOU CENTER YOURSELF BEFORE YOU BEGIN YOUR DAY?

I know I do. Which is why I'm going to spend a bit more time in the spiritual realm.

It's hard to pinpoint one influence or watershed moment that ignited my spiritual growth journey, but I think it was more of a general sense of exhaustion meets boredom meets terror. I was exhausted from feeling silenced, dismissed, and disregarded while at home. It was my senior year of high school, and I finally worked up the nerve to tell my first serious boyfriend about my childhood sexual abuse. We were watching TV in the basement like we always did, and out of nowhere, I started crying uncontrollably. I have no idea what triggered it or why it was at that moment lying on the big black pillows when I decided to share.

At any rate, I told him, and he urged me to tell my cousin. After telling her, she and her sister invited me to a woman's retreat at the family church. It was there that I finally let go and allowed myself to cry and turn to Spirit for answers and help. I wept, and they held me. Then my journey began. I didn't necessarily grow in that moment, but I recognized my responsibility and opportunity to put myself and my life together. In that moment, I realized my spiritual health was both my responsibility and my pathway toward liberation. There was the cracking open of my heart, ushering me into a kind of spiritual journey I couldn't have imagined.

From there, I went on to college, a liberal arts PWI (predominantly white institution) in Virginia. I remained with that boyfriend through the first year, as he was the best and most trusted human I had on earth. He listened to me, he believed me, and he didn't judge me for what I shared. By sophomore year, we broke up but remained friends, and I had time to truly bridge the gap between childhood and adulthood. As I began

NOTES

allowing myself to feel emotions I'd bottled up for nearly two decades, depression sank in, and I stopped playing softball—which would mark the first year since I was four that I didn't play a sport—and quickly after quitting, I broke all the way down. I contemplated and planned suicide, checked myself into a hospital, and reached back out to my cousin for support. I thought that was the bottom for me, but it wasn't.

As part of my outpatient agreement, I had to commit to therapy. During my first few sessions, I let it all out; I told my therapist everything, and she cried harder than I did. At one point, she said it was time to bring my father into our sessions. I called him from my dorm room to invite him to my next session, and he immediately refused to come. I inquired several times about his reason for not wanting to attend, and he finally responded by telling me he wanted to have a career in politics one day and thought seeing a therapist would damage his chances. That was the bottom for me. My heart sank; my throat dried and tightened. However, breakthrough happened. I, for the first time, raised my voice and expressed my anger. I shouted about whether he'd have better chances if I'd been successful in killing myself. I shouted about him not being present in my life, for prioritizing work and other people, and for not keeping me safe. I shouted, wailed, and released emotions I didn't know I had. He made the next therapy session.

Often, it's the response to abuse or neglect that hurts us more than the abuse or neglect itself. So many of us are processing our own compounded and state-sanctioned trauma that it's extremely difficult to know what we've numbed, stuffed, processed, transferred, or healed. We all do the best we can from the knowledge and consciousness we have at the time. Caring for our spiritual health allows us to raise our consciousness behind our beliefs, values, and actions and make more deliberate choices. We are all spiritual beings having a human experience, and a very sick collective consciousness addicted to white supremacy and patriarchy disproportionately impacts those experiences. This sick collective consciousness has birthed a society with a superiority complex that exalts whiteness and patriarchy as the standard—two social constructs responsible for global discrimination, segregation, oppression, and violence. This struck a chord with many, and others may wonder how we went from abuse to white supremacy and patriarchy? Stick with me. Let me break this down.

NOTES

We each have our own consciousness or way we see ourselves in relation to the world around us. Our consciousness is nurtured through contemplation, influenced by the people we trust and those in power, and strengthened through spiritual self-discovery. The vibration of all of our individual consciousnesses combine to form an energetic collective consciousness. At the moment, a belief and subsequent sets of policies, governments, organizations, communities, churches, schools, etc. drive the collective consciousness that white people and straight men are superior and therefore should hold the power in all facets of the human experience. Such exaltation requires a set of behaviors to justify, protect, and perpetuate both constructs that include, but are not limited to, violence, rape, discrimination, collusion, and oppression. As spiritual beings having a human experience, we are all tasked with making meaning of how the sick collective consciousness affects our own consciousness and how we view ourselves in relation to the world around us.

As a young adult in college acknowledging and reconciling my sexual abuse and depressed state for the first time, I viewed my experiences as a part of who I am. It deeply affected my sense of worthiness and self-esteem. I didn't have the consciousness or the tools to separate my abuse and my depressive state from who I am and was created to be. Trauma convolutes our consciousness and sends our bodies into fight or flight modes. If we don't deliberately heal ourselves, we can live in that convoluted state for the rest of our lives. Many of us do. I call it sleepwalking. As Solange put it, we drink it away, sex it away, work it away, etc.[5] We go into autopilot, not realizing we're unconsciously embodying and enacting the very same belief system supported by the sick collective consciousness. It becomes a vicious cycle.

As I ventured through my first therapy experience, I also started reading books about spirituality and various religions. I grew up in the Baptist church and while I enjoyed the cultural and familial aspects, I can't say I was growing spiritually and many of the patriarchal teachings didn't speak to me. My intuition kept guiding me to be open and learn more, so I read several books and articles about metaphysics, spiritual laws, ancient African spiritual traditions, contemplative practices, emotional intelligence, and leadership. Synthesizing is one of my superpowers and I quickly noticed a few key trends across all the texts I read over the course of about twenty years.

5. Solange, "Cranes in the Sky," Track 4 on *A Seat at the Table*, released 30 Sept. 2016.

NOTES

(Yes, I'm that friend who has a book or article for just about anything.) Those trends included the following:

- We're spiritual beings having a human experience. Our True self represents the divine in us, and our egos represent the human parts of us.

- We live in an abundant Universe but are governed by a pervasive scarcity mindset.

- Each of us can speak to and form a relationship with God, or whatever we call the divine energy, at any given moment and without the assistance of anyone else.

- There are several paths for spiritual growth, no one path is superior to the other.

- God lives within all of us.

- God is love.

- Our lives are a reflection of our consciousness; as some put it "what you focus on, grows."

Most spiritual books end with that last piece: "Our lives are a reflection of our consciousness." This is dangerous as a singular statement because it disregards the disproportionate negative impact the sick collective consciousness has on individuals who don't identify as white or as a man. It can make people part of marginalized groups made to feel like they somehow caused discrimination, oppression, and racism to be present in their lives or that they are responsible for "overcoming" it. Our lives are a combination of our own *and* the sick collective consciousness.

OUR LIVES ARE A COMBINATION OF OUR OWN *AND* THE SICK COLLECTIVE CONSCIOUSNESS.

It's through spiritual self-discovery that we learn how to know ourselves separately from the sick collective consciousness. Many of us experience this as making the deliberate choice to live authentically. We feel that nudge that says it's time to wake up from our sleepwalking state and live in an elevated state. We begin discovering and loving ourselves in fresh ways. We open and soften to alternative pathways to knowing our divine selves, and we begin experiencing more joy and abundance than we have before.

"Be authentic" is one of our organization's values, and we say to lead authentically means to lead in harmony

NOTES

with our values and purpose—while maintaining a genuine openness to diverse perspectives and a curious presence with those around us. Authenticity inspires trust, commitment, cohesion, and vulnerability among teams. When teams function in this elevated state, the results they produce are both outstanding and sustainable. We support our leaders in (re)discovering their authentic leadership voices and styles, and this journey begins with a commitment to spiritual self-discovery.

So yes, that was a long-winded answer to why the spiritual bucket is more important than any other self-care bucket. It's the one that holds the key to your healing, and it's much more than a set of practices; it's the opportunity to operate within an elevated consciousness.

Remember that Strong Black Woman Schema I mentioned? Research tells us the antidote to the schema is self-compassion. Self-compassion is defined as viewing oneself with kindness and nonjudgment while suffering, during perceived failure, or feelings of inadequacy.[6] Self-compassion has three components:

---

6. Neff, K. D. (2003b). "Self-Compassion: An Alternative Conceptualization of a Healthy Attitude toward Oneself," *Self and Identity*, vol. 2, 85–102. Published online 24 Sept. 2010, Taylor & Francis Online, https://doi.org/10.1080/15298860309032.

1. Self-kindness—being comforting to oneself in times of pain.
2. Common humanity—recognizing one's suffering is part of the larger human experience.
3. Mindfulness—holding one's painful feelings and thoughts in mindful awareness.

If you're wondering what spiritual practices you should begin with, I invite you to begin with those that allow you to experience self-compassion. This will look different for people based upon their context and interests. For some this can appear as doing a loving kindness meditation with frequency or it could also look like forgiving yourself for sleepwalking. It can look like opening yourself up to perceive your experience of pain in a new way or from the perspective of the perpetrator. For example, my father's decision to put his political aspirations before my needs is a decision supported by the sick collective consciousness and he likely wasn't consciously aware of how he was betraying himself or me. He was operating at the level of consciousness he had at the time and may not have trusted himself to be fully aware of what happened to me and what role he played. It likely terrified him. Through self-compassion

---

NOTES

for what I experienced, I can now strengthen my capacity for compassion for him and be in a place of forgiveness. Practicing self-compassion can also look like expressing your anger or frustration or simply taking a nap. Do what feels kind to you.

DO WHAT FEELS KIND TO YOU.

Many of you might even need to think of what you would do for loved ones before it becomes a habit for you to put yourselves first.

Right spiritual practices mean right for you and your lifestyle. What may bring one person ease may cause another anxiety. For example, one of my clients takes great joy in swimming in a cold lake every morning. She experiences feeling more alive and energized for her day. When I think about all I would need to do to prepare for work after my swim and all the time I would need to put into washing and styling my hair, that brings me anxiety. I would think about that "time lost" before, during, and after my swim. Then I would feel guilty about not knowing how to swim as smoothly as I would like. You get the point.

I have another client who takes joy in noting which animals and insects cross her path each day. She takes delight in searching for their spiritual significance and applying it to her life. Each time, she picks up a message of guidance and comfort. She inspired me to try the practice as well. The other day, a bee flew into my car while at a stoplight. It flew into the driver's window side and hovered in front of my face for several seconds and then flew away.

Bees are a symbol of hard work, sustainability, and life. They're also a symbol of the sun, community, and celebration. Bees remind us to be productive in our daily lives and give back to the world in the best ways possible. They often show up when we get sidetracked from a goal and need to become more focused. This happened during a time when I got sidetracked from writing this book. For about two weeks, instead of writing this book, I wrote proposals, onboarded new clients, welcomed children into my home for a learning pod, served on boards, got my kids off to a somewhat strong remote learning start, prioritized my health, and rested. As I moved through these other roles I play, I started feeling guilty about deprioritizing my writing. Then the bee showed up to remind me that I'm on the "right" path, my path. Now you get to choose yours.

Adopting self-care as a mindset requires a commitment to live authentically. The very act of making that

NOTES

decision is a radical act of self-care that will continually unlock new levels of joy and liberation. Ask yourself:

- "What do I need?"

- "What would support me to live like fear isn't an option?"

Take a few, slow breaths and jot down what immediately comes to mind. Expect to flow into the next version of you with more ease.

Chapter 3
TELL THE TRUTH

I WAS WHAT SOME WOULD CALL A TOMBOY GROW-
ing up. I wanted trucks instead of dolls, exercise equip-
ment instead of dollhouses. I ran outside with the boys
during my visits to Grandma's house, and I loved to compete—still do. It's hard to know whether that was innate
or because I craved the attention of my father. He would
light up at my achievements in gymnastics, softball, and
basketball. I excelled in most athletic arenas, and I liked
the sound of him bragging about me to his friends and
colleagues. I was a true #sisterinsweat.

I cared just as much about my team winning as I
did about me performing well or winning a particular
event. I always did my best—always. I didn't know any
other way. It wasn't until I started managing people for
the first time that I realized everyone didn't operate this
way. To better manage others, I decided that I needed
to wear pants suits at work every day for folks to take
me seriously. In my defense, it was the early to mid-
2000s, but still. Pants suits were my swag then, but if
I'm honest, I wanted to wear more skirts and dresses

and just thought it wouldn't cut it. I was filling a white man's shoes and thought I had to follow that script as closely as possible.

I would learn much later, several leadership positions later, that my femininity is a big part of my power, and when you couple femininity with Blackness and a determination to thrive, you have magic. What you get is a leader who wants everyone to thrive in both the process and the outcome—who understands what it feels like to get marginalized and will go to lengths to ensure everyone is seen, valued, heard, and elevated. You have a soul-filled leader who can easily hear what isn't said, who can see the potential in people others have written off, and who can genuinely connect with a wide range of individuals. You also have a leader who has stamina; a leader who has had to develop immense amounts of patience, grace, and resolve. You have a leader who has had to earn every morsel of elevation, who has been underestimated from the beginning and who has an arsenal of creativity, drive, and love ready to be unleashed and transformed into unprecedented outcomes. You have an *IndigoWoman*.

YOU HAVE AN INDIGOWOMAN.

NOTES

Much like I did in the early to mid-2000s to discover my authentic leadership style and voice, *IndigoWomen* must continually ask themselves about their relationship with the masculine and feminine manifestations of their personalities. Questions that support this kind of self-discovery include the following:

- What influences how you show up and what energy you lean into?

- Is this a conscious choice?

- What would happen if you more deliberately leaned into one more than the other?

- What comes naturally to you?

We all possess beautiful energies and both traditional masculine and feminine energies have the power to have a significant, positive impact on ourselves and those we lead and love. Most of my clients tend to credit their masculine attributes for their success in leadership or entrepreneurship, and they, particularly my cis and straight clients, tend to also blame those attributes for not being as successful in their love lives. This is another area where it's important to examine not only your own experience and will, but to also examine the impact the sick collective consciousness has had on how we show up. It can be hard for us to know what our truth is when it comes to masculine and feminine energies because the sick collective consciousness attempts to answer this question for us. Patriarchal ideology asserts a binary and restrictive set of characteristics for what it means to be a woman or man, guiding many to suppress what comes naturally to them. Committing to live and lead in an awakened state requires us to rearrange and reexamine our relationship with socially constructed norms for gender.

COMMITTING TO LIVE AND LEAD IN AN AWAKENED STATE REQUIRES US TO REARRANGE AND REEXAMINE OUR RELATIONSHIP WITH SOCIALLY CONSTRUCTED NORMS FOR GENDER.

Many of us have done the StrengthsFinder assessment, where you answer a battery of questions about your values and preferences, then it churns out your top five strengths. Prior to making the deliberate decision to be and live authentically, responsibility was one of my top five. It made sense. I grew up early, was the big cousin who always babysat the younger crew, was always captain of my sports teams,

NOTES

and was even the grade team leader during my first year of teaching at age twenty-one. I took each role seriously and had a deep care for those I was responsible for leading. I felt responsible for them. I bought into the notion that "the buck stops with me." I owned their mistakes and propped them up; when they took a misstep, it was my fault and when they succeeded, it was then that I knew I was doing a good job.

What I later learned was that this masculine, age-old approach often led me to overemphasize or inflate my sense of importance. I missed opportunities to trust other people's instincts. I attempted to control outcomes and, in the process, grew exhausted, overworked, and overwhelmed. Channeling my energy toward getting and being still taught me to trust in an energy greater than myself.

Pointedly, I alone could not make any goal or vision come to fruition. I had to trust Spirit, trust the Spirit in me, and trust the Spirit in others. My confidence slowly and gradually grew. I let go of the outcome and focused on me, what I was communicating, and how I was leading.

POINTEDLY, I ALONE COULD NOT MAKE ANY GOAL OR VISION COME TO FRUITION. I HAD TO TRUST SPIRIT, TRUST THE SPIRIT IN ME, AND TRUST THE SPIRIT IN OTHERS.

This shift in how I defined success helped me thrive as a leader. Success isn't just about achieving something; it's also about the journey you took to get there. The "whatever it takes" mindset lacks the intentionality needed to arrive at experiences and outcomes that benefit everyone, especially the most marginalized. "Whatever" encompasses what will benefit the person driving the intended result. The end doesn't always justify the means, especially not for those most marginalized. The experience or journey in an endeavor is just as important as the result.

IndigoWomen are open to letting go of words that once inspired us and were written in and for a different time like, "Without struggle, there is no progress." Struggle and sacrifice aren't always necessary for progress or success. We can thrive with ease, grace, and more patience. When success is about both the journey and the result, we open the path for alternative possibilities, ideas, and perspectives. We discover there are always multiple ways to manifest a particular outcome. We also discover that Spirit flows with our decisions. We don't just build things, we birth them. We go from forcing to allowing and from controlling to trusting. We go from exhaustion to invigoration, and we nurture the kinds of relationships

NOTES

that continue to feed our minds, bodies, and souls—the kinds of relationships that call us higher.

The following exercise has supported many of my former clients to gain clarity around what success really looks and sounds like for them. Set aside about an hour and expect to be divinely guided.

SUCCESS RE-IMAGINATION EXERCISE

1. Take at least three deep breaths.
2. Set an intention to joyfully expand your definition of success.
3. Grab a piece of paper and draw a line down the middle.
4. On the left-hand side, draw or paste images and write words that represent your past understanding of what success means. Do this without judgment and invite curiosity.
5. Set an intention for a new definition of success to surface. Set a timer for 10 minutes and meditate with that intention in mind.

6. On the right-hand side, draw images and write words that represent your emerging understanding of success. Set a 30-minute timer and see what emerges. Again, do this without judgment and invite curiosity.

7. Record your thoughts in your journal regarding what you notice about each side. (i.e., What are the trends? What is the common thread? What about the images feel good?)

8. With this new awareness, set an intention to grow, learn, and succeed with grace and ease. Hold your desired outcomes lightly and be open to those outcomes shifting or changing in unexpected ways.

When I did this exercise many years ago, I noticed the left-hand side of my collage had several images that were masculine. They looked industrial and linear. I had images of people in a race, in various forms of hierarchical order, and symbols of external success like degrees or certificates. The right side had softer and rounder images of people dancing, laughing, relaxing, and blossoming. When I took the StrengthsFinder assessment several years later, my Responsibility strength went away

NOTES

and Self-Assurance replaced it. This strength speaks to a trust in my intuition and inner wisdom. This is the kind of divine, feminine energy our world is screaming out for. My confidence doesn't come from a "track record of success"; it comes from the ability to be lovingly present at any moment. When present, I hear what isn't being said and see what most don't see. I notice opportunities missed by many and see beyond someone's misguided comment and into what the moment is teaching all of us. I don't have to put forth an immense amount of effort—many times my presence is enough.

Redefining success can be very uncomfortable for some; it has certainly been for many of my former clients. Many of them have talked about how they have the masculine aspects of success to thank for the leadership positions they've earned. They describe the complexity of feeling proud of what they've been able to achieve while also being aware of the relationships and parts of themselves they may have sacrificed. For many of them, this route is the only example they've seen. They learned you have to be "twice as good" to be considered half as qualified. They've also experienced and observed that sentiment to be true through watching friends or colleagues who didn't buy into the same success paradigm get looked over for promotions or not considered for other career-advancing opportunities like board service or being selected as a speaker at various conferences. We live in a current paradigm, the sick collective consciousness, that equates hard work with sacrifice. Sacrifice suggests there aren't enough resources to go around, and we must compete for and force a particular outcome. It's born out of a fear-based scarcity mindset.

IndigoWomen understand we live in an abundant Universe with enough resources for everyone to thrive. A scarcity mindset teaches that we must work constantly or make a series of sacrifices to receive what we desire. Many believe in an abundant mindset in theory and in spirit, but have a tough time making the shift to actually living and leading through that paradigm. A question that may support folks in making the shift from a scarcity mindset to an abundant one when it comes to manifesting success is: What about how I naturally show up scares me?

WHAT ABOUT HOW I NATURALLY SHOW UP SCARES ME?

In most leadership dilemmas that my clients face, there's a truth about themselves that they've yet to accept for one reason or another. Sometimes it's because they fear what the truth will require them to do or be. Other

NOTES

times it's because they've just never created the stillness required to explore what might be beneath the surface. What we discover together is that the common cliché rings true every time: The truth will set you free.

The rebirthing process is an invitation to reexamine and transform our purpose(s) for our leadership and lives. We are dynamic beings with ever-evolving circumstances, beliefs, values, and desires. What we focus upon needs to shift with who we are becoming. At the beginning of this section, I invited you to set an intention around what you'd like to learn, experience, and manifest in your life and leadership.

- What emerged?

- What do you now know about yourself that you didn't know before?

Pause a bit to answer those questions before continuing onto the next phase. Allow those shifts to settle.

When we discover and declare a grander vision for our leadership and lives, we invite both new triumphs and new challenges. In order to stay the course, *IndigoWomen* remain rooted in their compelling why and adjust their strategy accordingly. Resetting, the next part of the R3 Method™, is all about getting clear about why you want to realign your leadership and life with your JCC and how you can make that happen. Let's get to it.

NOTES

Part II

RESET

L – Lead from the Center

E – Eliminate Control, Attachments, and Assumptions

T – Trust and Forgive Yourself and Others

LET YOURSELF BE FREE.

DECLARING A GRANDER VISION AND PURPOSE FOR our lives is exhilarating. It also means that new challenges are on the horizon. To keep that same energy of exhilaration going, it's important to proactively reset or prime your mindset and environmental conditions to meet and tackle the new challenges. When women in the *IndigoWoman Group Coaching Experience* mention having difficulty with procrastination or other symptoms of imposter syndrome, oftentimes we discover that one reason they were experiencing those feelings of inadequacy is because their reasons for their goals or desired outcomes aren't compelling enough. I love what Reverend Michael Beckwith says about this: "The pain pushes, until the vision pulls." Your "Why" must drive what you'd like to accomplish. Most leadership and self-help books stop here, asserting one's mindset alone will pull them toward their vision without acknowledging the context and conditions leaders—in this case Black women—are operating within. This section is an invitation to examine and reset both your mindset *and* conditions necessary for your reimagined definition of success. Here are some trending questions from former clients that inspired this part of the R3 Method™:

- As a Black leader in a predominately white organization, how do I know whether I've betrayed myself or other Black/marginalized people at my workplace or in my life?

- How do I quickly gain the trust of a racially diverse staff when taking over from a white leader who created and enforced racist practices that I, too, once enforced?

- How do I lead people and teams who don't value self-care or sustainability as much as quantitative results?

- How do I authentically network and build relationships with white and non-Black people who influence or contribute to my work in some way—without assimilating to white dominant cultural norms?

- How do I interrupt my practice of perfectionism when perfectionism is the expectation at work?

- How do I disagree and engage in healthy conflict without being labeled an Angry Black Woman? Is this even possible?

- How can I more effectively and comfortably delegate when I know that the margin for error is much smaller for me as a Black woman?

- How do I address and interrupt interpersonal and institutional microaggressions at work?

- How do I make peace with the ways in which I've betrayed or dishonored myself?

NOTES

- How do I center self-care when I don't have a work environment that supports centering self-care?

Sis, you're going to need a refill on that favorite beverage and an adjustment in your seat. Take a few deep breaths and intend to usher in an expanded way to breakthrough inevitable setbacks, challenges, and opportunities for growth on the horizon. Let's get it.

Chapter 4

LEAD FROM THE CENTER

AUDRE LORDE SAYS, "WHEN WE SPEAK WE ARE afraid our words will not be heard or welcomed. But when we are silent, we are still afraid. So it is better to speak."[7] Whether invited or not, centered or not, our voices have the power to raise consciousness. When you get that nudge to pause, shift, or ignite an important conversation, speak up. Often our energy leaks through missed opportunities to say the thing, do the thing, and honor our truth. We are not in this world; the world is in us.

While the rebirthing process is all about gaining clarity about what you want, the reset process is about gaining clarity around why you want it. When you're leveling up, usually there are whispers about what we're called to do before we understand why. Many of us have been in leadership roles long enough to understand that why

---

7. Lorde, Audre, *The Black Unicorn: Poems* (United Kingdom: Norton, 1995).

we do something is what will keep us in it when it gets tough. It's our why that will motivate us to adopt and honor new habits, mindsets, and ways of being. Once we know our why, we're free to be courageous and set new limits for ourselves.

Honoring and caring for ourselves includes asserting ourselves and expressing ourselves in our unique way. Often my clients would express being exhausted, thinking it was because of the volume of work they had while running their households. While their lives were certainly full, once we dug a bit deeper, we discovered there were patterns in their lives with sprinklings of tiny moments where they made themselves smaller, hid, shied away from sharing their perspective, or opted to conceal their genuine emotions. These patterns happened both personally and professionally and ranged from situations of not sharing their dissenting view about a new organizational initiative to not revealing their budding feelings for a new romantic partner. When they shared such moments, their shoulders raised a bit, their eyes diverted downward more frequently, and they often spoke with long pauses. I was picking up on the draining sensations that surfaced for them by just talking about it, and I could only imagine what they experienced when in those moments. I was witnessing delayed moments of vulnerability.

I WAS WITNESSING DELAYED MOMENTS OF VULNERABILITY.

Many of us have read and heard Brené Brown, author of *Daring Greatly* and other great books, talk extensively about the importance and power of vulnerability. Those who have, love us some Brené Brown, don't we? *What is that about?!* I digress. But seriously, it's in those vulnerable moments when we take leaps of faith in ourselves and others. We trust our judgment around when, how, and with whom to share, and we trust the receivers to hold space for us with ease and grace. It's a dance of all dances. You can't plan the next moves; you can't control the outcome. You can only go with the flow and see what unfolds. In this case, it's usually deepened relationships, creative solutions, and experiences of love. Then there are those other times when the receiver misunderstands, rejects, or misinterprets us, and we want to fold into a ball and never come back out. These are universal experiences.

What's not as universal, but common for us, is the additional risk that being vulnerable can present. For example, I've heard clients in the past say things like, "The margin for error for me is so much smaller than my

NOTES

78

white or non-Black colleagues. If I'm open about what I'm grappling with, my competence will get questioned even further than it already has." They're telling the truth. Their organization's data was riddled with disproportionate numbers of Black women leaving the organization, not being promoted, or not represented in positions of power. When you add the white supremacy culture trait of fear of conflict, the conditions for Black women to be vulnerable are rocky at best. This has been the case since Black women could join the workforce and has led to a pervasive internalization and transference of racism— most of which happens unconsciously.

Donna Bivens, a diversity, inclusion, and equity consultant and trainer, says, "Internalized racism occurs in a racist system when a racial group oppressed by racism supports the supremacy and dominance of the dominating group by maintaining or participating in the set of attitudes, behaviors, social structures and ideologies that undergird the dominating group's power."[8] When we do this, we've internalized the sick collective consciousness, or whiteness construct, as the standard to

---

8. Bivens, Donna, "What Is Internalized Racism?" in Maggie Potapchuk, et al, *Flipping the Script: White Privilege and Community Building* (United States: MP Associates, 2005), 45–46.

measure ourselves. For example, many of us have been explicitly told or we've learned through experience that we must work twice as hard, speak impeccable standard English, dress conservatively, and adopt many other white dominant norms. Proximity to whiteness gets rewarded through job attainment, promotions, social and political capital, power, and money. This dynamic creates scarce conditions where Black women make false choices between exhibiting a whitewashed version of their authentic selves and concealing their perspectives and emotions. When this sick collective consciousness prevails, some Black women unconsciously transfer this racism onto their very own. Bivens breaks down that the transmission process includes the attitudes, perspectives, beliefs, values, and assumptions that lead the members of subordinate groups to act in ways that consciously or unconsciously support or collude with the systems of oppression that target them. It may also include the transmission of psychological, emotional, and behavioral patterns of internalized oppression, or the conditions that would cause the development of such patterns.

There are times I look back at my teaching and school leadership days and think about ways I was upholding and perpetuating practices and policies that were inherently

NOTES

racist. While I may not have necessarily created said policies and practices or even had the consciousness to know they were oppressive, I implemented them because I thought it was "best practice" and it was expected of me. Internalized racism looks like accepting a white construct as right or the only way, and there I was transferring racist systems and ideologies that were not in the best interest of the very people who looked like me. *I'm still taking a breath.* That's a devastating realization; so devastating that I understand why some decide to sleepwalk.

Resetting is partly about deepening our self-awareness about ways in which we've betrayed ourselves through unhealed internalized racism. This level of healing, truth telling, and release gives us courage to be able to be more vulnerable in our workplaces and with those we lead and love in our personal lives. There are very few places where we can go to do such healing work, which is one reason I was called to cocreate the *IndigoWoman Group Coaching Experience.* This is our work that only we can do—together.

RESETTING IS PARTLY ABOUT DEEPENING OUR SELF-AWARENESS ABOUT WAYS IN WHICH WE'VE BETRAYED OURSELVES THROUGH UNHEALED INTERNALIZED RACISM.

Something we say in our *IndigoWomen* community is that resetting is about going from leading from the margins to leading from the center. We're all part of at least two marginalized groups, which means the sick collective consciousness is disproportionately present in our personal and professional lives. This also means we need to support each other in new and varied ways of separating our own consciousness from the sick collective consciousness and becoming more authentic, transformative leaders. While the sick collective consciousness may try to push us to the margins, the truth is we are firmly in the center of our own lives and in this world. When we reconnect with our own consciousness, we remember and channel our power, and its impact is seismic.

To support *IndigoWomen* in resetting both their mindsets and conditions for reimagined success, I leaned into my teaching and school leadership background and created a framework called the PVT. (Yes, inspired in part by PYT—Pretty Young Thing. *I'm corny, ya'll!* It fits and now you'll remember it too, so let's flow with it.) The PVT supports leaders in tapping into their unique superpowers to lead in ways only they can. Let me break this down. You may want to grab a highlighter, pen, and journal.

NOTES

While your JCC represents what you do as you lead, your PVT represents why you lead. Remember, your "why" is what anchors you as a leader. It's what you call upon when you make mistakes, hit roadblocks, navigate tough seasons, and catch yourself in negative talk loops. Part of caring for ourselves is revisiting and refining the why behind our leadership. Our "whys" fill our cups, activate new inspiration, inspire those we lead and love, and recommit us to the mission at hand.

The "P" in PVT is all about identifying your superpower. This can be identified by gaining clarity around who you are and what values govern how you show up and treat others. They represent your deeply held beliefs that both your journey and your ancestry influence. Your journey includes watershed and defining moments in both your personal and professional lives because they are integrated. How you show up in one part of your life represents how you show up in all parts of your life, and I've learned through coaching many powerful leaders that those who more closely integrate their values in both their personal and professional lives have deeper and more authentic relationships with loved ones and colleagues.

After reflecting on these different aspects of who you are, the next task is to sit back and tease out the thread of dopeness that shines through as your superpower. For example, my two leading values are love and liberation. I believe I'm here on earth to create ripple effects of love and liberation through my businesses, raising my children, friendships, coaching, leading, teaching, and now writing. I come from a line of women who are incredibly loving, ambitious, courageous, and nurturing. My journey is riddled with moments where I was called to lead by creating safe and vibrant spaces for people. The spaces ranged from classrooms, to schools, to boardrooms, to fields, to courts, to homes, and to now sacred virtual spaces. My superpower is creating spaces where people feel safe enough to be vulnerable and challenged enough to call themselves higher.

The "V" in PVT is about defining how and why you use your Voice. When we use our voice, we're communicating our deeply held beliefs about ourselves, people, and the world around us. It's important to both know what beliefs influence our voice and to hold those beliefs lightly enough to expand and change over time. Our beliefs and perspectives are driven by our life experiences,

NOTES

our schooling or learning processes, the media we consume, and the people in close proximity to us.

Our ability to understand and empathize with various perspectives hinges on our own range of diverse experiences and sets of people we invite into our lives. If we narrow the kinds of people and experiences within our lives, we make ourselves more prone to judge, dismiss, or discriminate against people who differ from us.

It's important to regularly reflect upon what and who influences your perspective and what else you could learn. How we position our voices pertains to what mediums, positions, or sectors we choose to amplify them. When we experience setbacks, it's important to allow ourselves time and space to experience and express the emotions that surface and then explore whether a pivot in positioning might be in order. For example, Stacey Abrams has a powerful TED Talk where she exemplifies the PVT in

> OUR ABILITY TO UNDERSTAND AND EMPATHIZE WITH VARIOUS PERSPECTIVES HINGES ON OUR OWN RANGE OF DIVERSE EXPERIENCES AND SETS OF PEOPLE WE INVITE INTO OUR LIVES.

action.[9] (Sis, google it and thank me later). She openly talked about how her life experiences in Georgia influenced her desire to run for governor. When she lost, instead of standing still, she repositioned her voice and started Fair Fight and arguably saved our democracy in the 2020 presidential election. Think about where you're positioned. Is it time to reposition or amplify your voice?

IS IT TIME TO REPOSITION OR AMPLIFY YOUR VOICE? It's important that we position ourselves in places that honor who we are and provide avenues for us to flex our JCC. We also use our voices through various initiatives and projects we take on. I've coached leaders in the past who thought they were ready to leave their organizations or abandon their businesses because they got bored or felt like they were treading water. Through the coaching process, many of them realized that they'd fallen into a bit of a sleepwalking state at work and weren't challenged enough. I invited them to think about what bringing creativity and innovation could look like in their roles, and many of them created and later led new

9. Abrams, Stacey, "3 questions to ask yourself about everything you do," TEDWomen, Dec. 2018, https://www.ted.com/talks/stacey_abrams_3_questions _to_ask_yourself_about_everything_you_do/details.

NOTES

initiatives that fulfilled them and had an impact. To affirm how you'd like to use your voice, complete this sentence as if it is already true:

I use my voice at work and home in the following ways _____ for the purpose of _____, and it makes me and others feel _____.

The "T" in PVT stands for the most precious resource we have, our Time. To know me is to know I don't play with my time. I mean, my love language is Quality Time. Time is everything! In this context, this is an invitation to get clear about how you use your time, why you use it the way you do, and the conditions in which you flow throughout life. Let's begin with the conditions—your environment. Our physical space can shift our mood and it's important to proactively cocreate the mood necessary for you being and giving your best.

WHERE DO YOU SPEND MOST OF YOUR TIME, AND IS IT CONDUCIVE TO BEING PRODUCTIVE, CREATIVE, AND FREE?

Where do you spend most of your time, and is it conducive to being productive, creative, and free?

Many of us work from home now. Do you have dedicated space for doing your work and contemplative practices? What colors bring you joy, and do they somehow surround you? Sis, we're royalty. Does your space make you feel that way? If you don't work from home, how can you shift or advocate for the resources to shift the physical space where you work?

Next, think about how you create and bring your JCC to life. When I was in my sleepwalking years, I completely let go of the athletic side of me. Athletics were a big part of my childhood and early adulthood, and I often say, saved my life. It's through sports that I gained the body love and awareness that still serves me today. I made some of my most important friendships through athletics, and it was my first and most influential introduction into leadership. Deeper than that, through my own coaching process with my leadership coach, I learned some of my greatest ideas come after working out or playing. So, I purchased a treadmill desk to walk while I create and work. It tends to raise my vibration and keeps me in flow. Think back to when you've had great ideas or "aha" moments. What were the conditions that led to those ideas or new creations?

WHAT WERE THE CONDITIONS THAT LED TO THOSE IDEAS OR NEW CREATIONS?

NOTES

Intentionally recreate those conditions so that you can more readily and frequently maintain a state of flow.

While the creative process is about how you create, creative expression is about what you create. What do you spend time creating and manifesting? How might you take a more creative approach to your leadership role?

HOW MIGHT YOU TAKE A MORE CREATIVE APPROACH TO YOUR LEADERSHIP ROLE?

Many of us are artists and either don't realize it or have put that side of ourselves to the side to support our households and those we lead. We may need to expand our definition of creativity. We're in the process of creating anytime we are expressing our voice, solving a problem, or creating an experience. If you don't already, think of your role as an opportunity to be creative and see what new ideas emerge.

Finally, how do you prioritize your time—both in terms of what you do and with whom? Let's begin with focusing on the people who get to be in your presence. Many of us have heard the saying, "You are the sum of the five people you spend most of your time with." You good? Take stock, Sis. If you find yourself spending too much time with people who don't fill your cup or otherwise support you, it may be time to set an intention

to attract people who better align with your consciousness. Then, pay attention to and try new avenues for
getting to know more people. Sign up for a meet-up
group, course of interest, or get out and enjoy a hobby
you haven't tried in a long time. There may be someone
there who will support your level-up season in ways you
never thought possible.

When I ask clients to reflect upon what they spend
their time doing, a pattern of "doing it all" often
emerges. Before our coaching engagement gets under-
way, they often have very scheduled and full calendars
with little time for breaks, thinking, rest, or time for
those they love. They often have tasks on their calendars that represent roles and responsibilities of a few
other colleagues—in addition to their own. Somewhere
along the way they've either not delegated or absorbed
tasks they previously delegated. This dynamic usually
emerges because of one or any combination of the following circumstances:

- When they delegated a task, they weren't
  explicit enough about the criteria or vision
  for success.

NOTES

- The person they delegated it to needed more coaching, time, and support along the way— and sooner after the task was delegated.

- The task they delegated is time sensitive and high stakes and they realized later that they didn't have enough time to coach the person to bring it to completion.

- The person they delegated it to is afraid to disappoint them, so they smoothly gave the task back to my client.

That last one is often in my clients' blind spot because it appeals to their focus on getting the task done "correctly" and the illusion that it will get done quicker if they just do it. While taking a task back may provide a short-term solution, in the long run, it gets in the way of building the leadership capacity of others and providing sustainability for my clients. When examining Time within the PVT, it's important to take a time inventory of sorts. Look at your calendar and note how much of your time is spent reacting vs. proactively creating or coaching. What do you spend most of your time doing, and will those tasks best contribute to you achieving your goals and flowing within your JCC? How much time do you spend building the capacity of those you lead?

Knowing your PVT deepens your self-awareness in a way that you can more deliberately make, nurture, and manage the relationships within your life and career to better align with who you truly are and what you are here to do. It allows you to take up space in the most powerful and lasting way possible.

P My superpower is ...
- who you are
- values
- journey
- ancestry

V I use my voice at work by ...
for the purpose of ...
- beliefs
- perspective
- positioning
- initiatives

T I spend most of my time at work, and it makes me feel ...
- creative expression
- environment
- creative process
- priorities

VOICE

TIME

POWER

NOTES

NOTES

Chapter 5

ELIMINATE CONTROL, ATTACHMENTS, AND ASSUMPTIONS

I TEND TO ATTRACT CLIENTS WHO WOULD describe themselves as being at a crossroads. They have a sense that they need some sort of reset, but are not sure what it looks like. I call this being in the gap. You're in the gap between one way of being and the next one. We're going to explore how you know you're in the gap, and you'll become more aware of how eliminating control, attachments, and assumptions can pull you through the gap and into your desired state of being, leading, and living.

You know you're in the gap when you feel as if you're treading water. It can also feel as if you keep losing track of the days, of what time it is, and what exactly you're supposed to be doing. You kind of just look at your calendar, day-to-day, and go by what it says—not really putting much thought and intention into the big picture items. You're also in the gap when your life no longer works for you as it is, but you're not really sure what does. When Spirit speaks so loudly that He takes something pretty significant away (usually a job, an opportunity for advancement, maybe even a friendship), and then the loss makes room for what's on the other side . . . you're in the gap. However, sometimes we miss that, and we miss whatever opportunity will get us to the other side because we spend too long musing over that which no longer serves us.

HOWEVER, SOMETIMES WE MISS THAT, AND WE MISS WHATEVER OPPORTUNITY WILL GET US TO THE OTHER SIDE BECAUSE WE SPEND TOO LONG MUSING OVER THAT WHICH NO LONGER SERVES US.

You're in the gap when you struggle to make time for yourself, and you're so exhausted to where you're not sure what exactly is best. When suddenly you can't hear Spirit as clearly, and you're not quite sure whether this is the darkness of the soul or your mind playing tricks on you. When you're waffling between your true self and ego self, and it's really hard to stay above the fray and hear clearly, you're in the gap.

You're in the gap when you keep receiving the same constructive feedback and yet you haven't integrated it in any meaningful ways. Furthermore, you're in the gap

when you're not spending time with those most important to you and when you're prioritizing your responsibilities far over what your soul is crying out for.

When you're in that space, the gap, it's time to pause
and deepen your self-awareness.

Self-awareness has two components: how we perceive
our own emotions and how those emotions are perceived
by others. Most of us fall short with the second part of
that definition, but let's start with the first—knowledge
of our emotions or feelings. Our bodies often alert us to
feelings of anxiety or worry. Our faces get hot, we sweat,
our shoulders get tight, or maybe we stop or slow our
breathing because we feel threatened somehow. This is
the Amygdala Hijack, or as some put it, fight or flight
response. For many of us, our awareness ends there. We
buy books about reducing stress or managing our time
better. We buy into the notion that multitasking is unproductive and adopt new tools and strategies for getting things done. Then we find ourselves back at the beginning of our anxiety. Why? Because we met an obstacle manifesting below the

BECAUSE WE MET AN OBSTACLE MANIFESTING BELOW THE SURFACE WITH SURFACE-LEVEL STRATEGIES.

NOTES

surface with surface-level strategies. Therefore, we must dig deeper.

One way to dig deeper means letting go of our attachment to particular outcomes. Instead, we focus our attention on proactively deciding how we want to feel each day; and then intending to experience those feelings throughout the day—no matter what our calendars look like. What are those core-desired feelings that make you know you're alive? What are those feelings that make you feel like the best version of yourself? Your values are your best guides and could also be your core-desired feelings. For example, if you recall, two of my leading values are love and liberation, and I also desire to feel them each day. To discover your core-desired feelings, ask yourself questions like these:

- How do you want others to feel after being in your presence?

- Call your attention back to a time when you were in your zone, winning. How did you feel?

- Who do you admire, and how do they make you feel?

- What motivates or inspires you?

It's okay if you don't have the answers to all of those questions. Take them to your next meditation. You are likely gaining an awareness of how proactive or reactive you are in your life. Has life, until this point, been about responding to the needs and requests of others? In what ways have you directed your life? Is life happening to you or are you codesigning it? Take this as an invitation to have a more proactive than a reactive approach in living.

Let's get back to the other end of self-awareness: how others perceive and receive our emotions and how we show up. Many of my clients have gotten stuck in a gap because they unconsciously try to control how others perceive and receive them by overplanning, overworking, second-guessing their brilliance, concealing their ideas, or otherwise shrinking their PVT. This attempt to control is driven by a fear of not being enough. And here's the thing about this brand of fear—it can often be released through a series of courageous questions. Have we asked those we lead and love how they are receiving us? If rarely, then we are in the dark and that darkness cuts off an array of opportunities to know ourselves and others more deeply. We cut off the range of possibility for connection,

NOTES

understanding, and solutions. Consider asking those you lead and love:

- How do you experience me?

- In what ways do I inspire or motivate you?

- What can I do differently that would better communicate what I need from you?

- How can I better support you?

You may be sweating right now as you envision yourself asking those questions. You may also be thinking, "What if I don't inspire or motivate them, or what if I hear something I disagree with? How do I not appear defensive?" Simple: breathe. Get curious. Remember life is a series of at bats; swings are endless. You may learn about some unknown strike-outs; it's inevitable. You will also learn about ways you're winning with people you weren't aware of. It's when we release the need to control how and when we get out of the gap, and just commit to being curious about it, that we make our way to a new way of being.

In addition to releasing any attempts to control how others receive or perceive us, it's important to get curious about any attachments to old paradigms or sayings that once served us, but no longer do. For example, having a sense of urgency is a paradigm that can have dangerous implications. When I ask some of my clients when they're working through a tough season, "What is actually urgent?" they often pause, take a breath, cock their head to the side a bit, and then blurt out some version of, "I'm not really certain, but it just has to happen."

That pause of reconsideration supports them in realizing they are on autopilot. They've gotten entangled with the sick collective consciousness belief that perfection is the goal, more is better, faster is better, what we're focusing on is more important than it really is, and we are what we produce. When we slip into this consciousness, we frequently make up deadlines and rules. Who said that many items need to go on your to-do list for today? Who said you must reorganize your closet—today? Who said you must have a new policy in place by X holiday? What happens if you don't? Who set this standard in the first place? How can you renegotiate a previously made commitment?

NOTES

Let's define urgent: requiring immediate action or attention; done or arranged in response to a pressing or critical situation; earnest and persistent in response to a pressing situation. Outside of landing planes and resuscitating a human, what is really urgent? What must happen by a certain time? Few things, if we're honest. What would happen if we all looked at the arbitrary timelines we've set for ourselves and asked, is this really necessary? Who gets to decide what is urgent? Those are questions I'd like to see us ask more.

Most things we would categorize as urgent don't require an immediate response; they require an intentional one. They require a deliberate, careful approach that allows for multiple paths, not just one. We may need to ask ourselves, "What other ways could I approach this?"

Urgency feeds the ego's need to feel important, accomplished, and needed. Our true selves just want to be—simply exist in harmony. Harmony doesn't always get the adrenaline pumping; I know. That's because we've been conditioned to believe our natural state is one of fear and anxiety. I can't count the number

MOST THINGS WE WOULD CATEGORIZE AS URGENT DON'T REQUIRE AN IMMEDIATE RESPONSE; THEY REQUIRE AN INTENTIONAL ONE.

of times I hear the word "anxiety" mentioned in one day. On the one hand, it means we're normalizing mental health, which is great. However, on the other, it means we're normalizing anxiety. Urgency is like catnip to anxiety. Feeling anxious? Act! Go accomplish something, and fast! Folks, stop. Just stop and ask: Is this really urgent, and who gets to say it is?

IS THIS REALLY URGENT, AND WHO GETS TO SAY IT IS?

Being intentional means considering the implications that various decisions will have on people around us—individually and collectively. It means deliberately matching the mode of decision-making with the weight of the decision being made. It means asking yourselves, "Who isn't in the room? What don't I know about this topic? Am I the best person to make this decision? What micro-decisions are embedded in this decision?" Remember, you don't have to answer these questions by yourself. You have a team for a reason. Trust and ask them.

Another anxiety-booster is making assumptions. I always say, assumptions kill joy. I listen deeply and constructively to my clients when they describe their dilemmas, contexts, and pain points. I listen for patterns,

NOTES

emotions, and what's not said or expressed. Most explanations include both assertions and assessments.

Assertions are facts shared within an explanation and can be proven right or wrong. Assessments are opinions or assumptions based upon what the client experienced. For example, a client leading a network of schools once shared an experience where one of her white male board members repeatedly asked her what data she used to support a new initiative she implemented. She asserted that he asked her three times. Her assessment of the repeated questioning was that he was challenging her competence and being aversively racist. Avoiding assumptions becomes particularly hard when you're constantly on the receiving end of microaggressions and other oppressive practices. It's exhausting, painful, and sometimes debilitating.

It's important to note assumptions can be true, and when experiencing oppressive situations, they often are. Remember, facts can obscure truth. I affirmed my client's assessment and asked, "What's the gift in his questioning?" She paused and spoke about some new ideas that surfaced as she was answering his questions and thought of including someone else in her initiative she hadn't considered before. The tone in her voice softened;

she spoke more slowly and appeared more relaxed. Her initial anger and frustration slowly dissipated, and her focus was back on herself and her brilliant initiative. We then talked about how to address the board member's microaggression directly.

I want to be very clear, this isn't about finding the gift or silver lining in racism; it is about deliberately adopting a habit of shifting focus. How we feel about a situation gets influenced by the meaning we make of the situation. Leaders who hone the habit of extracting multiple meanings and teachings from a situation learn how to arrive at and transfer more creative and sustainable solutions.

IndigoWomen have to develop this skill to survive, let alone thrive. Our adaptation abilities are unmatched, making us tremendous assets to any team or organization. Our work is to remain in a state or mindset of self-care so we can have the emotional agility to recognize and interrupt microaggressions while also activating our self-management skills to extract what to focus on—all while honoring and advocating for ourselves. Whew. And when we select coaches and other support practitioners to assist us, it's critical they understand this nuance. Otherwise, they could make us feel like we're

NOTES

overreacting or dramatizing and not receive any guidance on how to navigate such situations.

Acknowledging pain isn't endorsing victimhood. I'll say that again: *Acknowledging pain isn't endorsing victimhood.*

Part of our healing process is acknowledging we're in pain in the first place. The sick collective consciousness is so pervasive, present, **ACKNOWLEDGING PAIN ISN'T ENDORSING VICTIMHOOD.** and ancient that we can sometimes trick ourselves into believing we just need to acquiesce, accept, or minimize it to survive. Clients have shared that prior to their coaching engagement with me, they were reluctant to share their painful oppressive experiences with anyone out of fear they would adopt a victim mindset or be perceived as such. Instead, they would dismiss, stuff, excuse, and internalize their experiences, and often were the ones who struggled the most with unconsciously transferring their internalized racism. Sis, get in community and partner with a coach or therapist who is equipped to hold space for the fullness of you. We need you healed, happy, and thriving.

While the gap can unearth some painful truths about ourselves, it's an invitation to grow and level up.

I've coached clients who have experienced this state for a few months and others a few years. Everyone's context is different, but what I can say from experience is that those who deliberately eliminate their attempts to control others and their circumstances, their attachments to beliefs and paradigms that no longer serve them, and their assumptions that could be draining their energy, tend to move through that state much faster. As mentioned before, breathe, get curious, and intend to thrive.

NOTES

Chapter 6

TRUST AND FORGIVE YOURSELF AND OTHERS

AS WE LET GO OF OLD THOUGHT PATTERNS, attachments, and assumptions, it's important to fill that space created with a greater capacity for uncertainty. When we're in the gap between where we've been and where we're headed, the lack of knowing exactly what to do, how to do it, and how long the gap will take, can be daunting. Any time we set an intention to reset or level-up in some way, we're being invited to trust and invest in ourselves in grand ways. It's this trust in ourselves that will increase our capacity to lead through uncertainty. We can't outperform the trust we place in ourselves. Our ability to achieve a goal or embody a purpose is directly linked to our self-belief.

How we live our lives—both personally and professionally—is feedback about our capacity to believe in ourselves. Evidence of this, or what I call the "faith index," is all around us. What we fill our calendars with, what we put in our bodies, who we befriend, and how we spend our money all tell us a little something about where we fall on the index. For *IndigoWomen*, developing a bold self-belief is absolutely paramount. Our willingness to take risks, stick to our strategic plans, and weather leadership storms depend on it. Faith is what is left standing in the depths of a crisis and is always what propels us back to victory.

In 2012 when I made the shift from the education sector to being an entrepreneur, I was presented with an opportunity to trust that I could transfer all I learned as a teacher, principal, and principal developer to founding my first business, Lead For Liberation (L4L) (formerly known as Teach To Lead (T2L)), specializing in organizational culture redesign. Oh, what a journey it has been. I don't think I've had to tap into another value more than trust. I leaned into what made me successful as an educator and for the first five years, successfully built an organization around meaningful work that brought me joy, and had a transformative impact on clients around the country. In year six, I fell out of love with it, and that scared me. I didn't expect that. What else was I going to do? It was my livelihood. It also didn't help, and was no coincidence at all, that we lost a clutch contract and were experiencing our rockiest financial year. I had to shift the two coveted full-time employees I worked so hard to hire back to part-time, and eventually I took on a full-time role to make ends meet. I fell into the gap and after releasing control, attachment, and assumptions all I had left was trust in myself.

Like in all gaps, I was presented with an opportunity to rebirth and reset by reflecting upon my JCC and PVT. Through that deeply reflective period, I discovered that it wasn't the core work I did at L4L that I fell out of love with, it was how my team and I were delivering it that was draining me. We were partnering with various organizations across the country with varying degrees of investment in the racial equity approach we took to our work. Our service delivery model required a high level of customization, making the work less sustainable and scalable. We'd reached a ceiling and my exhaustion blinded me from noticing the need for a shift in our business model. But I didn't give up.

As Spirit would have it, while in the gap, due to our emotional intelligence work at L4L, I was connected to Daniel Goleman's new organization, Goleman EI, and was selected as a meta-coach and faculty member responsible for certifying leaders in Emotional Intelligence

NOTES

Coaching globally. Goleman is one of the global pioneers in Emotional Intelligence. Not bad for a gap, huh? I met, coached, led, and learned alongside some incredible leaders in various sectors, and experienced a renewed and deepened trust in myself. This repositioning allowed me to take a look at L4L with fresh eyes and be innovative again. The common thread that binds the coaching I've done for the past fifteen years is emotional intelligence. I've always said that the muscle we're flexing when we're leading people who are different from us is emotional intelligence. However, the four domains of emotional intelligence written thirty-plus years ago don't represent the context and needs of various marginalized groups, particularly Black women. So, without an external request and on my own accord, I rewrote the domains through the lens of racial equity. Those refreshed domains serve as the backbone of the new business model at L4L and of the *IndigoWoman Group Coaching Experience.*

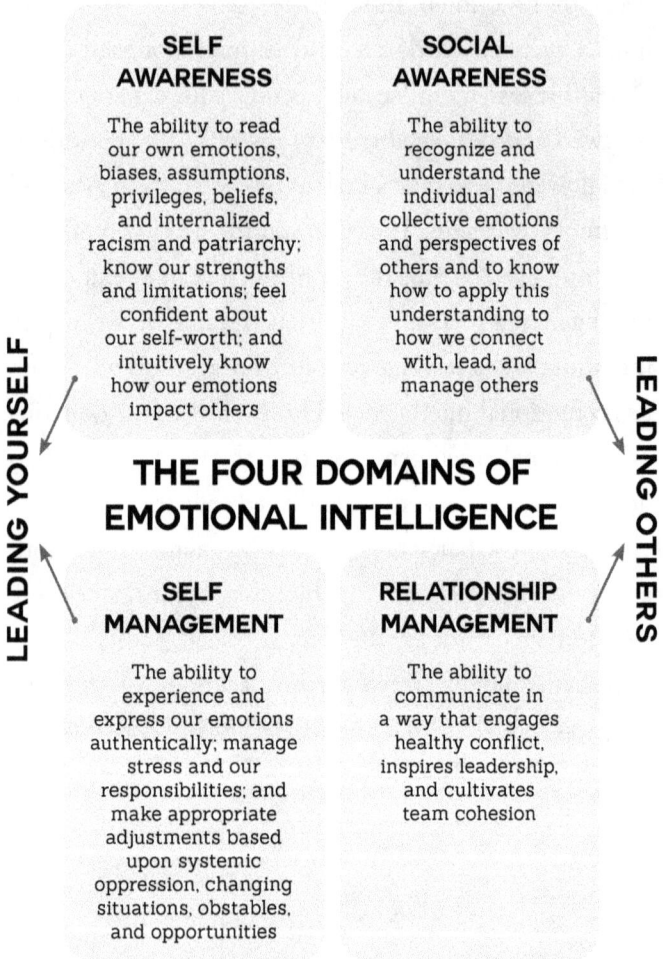

LEADING YOURSELF

LEADING OTHERS

SELF AWARENESS

The ability to read our own emotions, biases, assumptions, privileges, beliefs, and internalized racism and patriarchy; know our strengths and limitations; feel confident about our self-worth; and intuitively know how our emotions impact others

SOCIAL AWARENESS

The ability to recognize and understand the individual and collective emotions and perspectives of others and to know how to apply this understanding to how we connect with, lead, and manage others

THE FOUR DOMAINS OF EMOTIONAL INTELLIGENCE

SELF MANAGEMENT

The ability to experience and express our emotions authentically; manage stress and our responsibilities; and make appropriate adjustments based upon systemic oppression, changing situations, obstacles, and opportunities

RELATIONSHIP MANAGEMENT

The ability to communicate in a way that engages healthy conflict, inspires leadership, and cultivates team cohesion

NOTES

While this gap lasted about two long, stressful years, L4L experienced its most successful year to date, and the *IndigoWoman Group Coaching Experience* has already supported five cohorts of amazing executive/director level leaders and entrepreneurs from around the world.

I tell this story to illuminate what happens when we embrace trust in times of uncertainty. I didn't and couldn't have planned my partnership with Goleman EI. I didn't know that experience would inspire innovation in my first business and the birth of my second. I trusted Spirit, myself, and the relationships and solid work I'd built over the years. Another key mindset shift that I made during this phase was that I forgave myself for falling short. I was devastated by having to let my employees go and experienced guilt and shame along the way. Through my own coaching sessions with my coach, I realized that I slipped into an old pattern of taking on more than my fair share of responsibility. To break back out of that mindset, I committed to more deliberately practicing gratitude by beginning each day journaling about three things I was grateful for and ending each day journaling about three big wins I experienced. It was this practice and shift in mindset that paved the way for my bounce back.

Trust, forgiveness, and gratitude are powerful mindset-shifting practices. When you find yourself struggling to trust yourself in the midst of uncertainty, ask yourself what you need to forgive yourself for and write it down. Release the regret that things unfolded the way that they did, release the circumstance to a higher power, and intend to take the lessons with you. Be grateful for the journey and be present for what unexpected gifts are buried within the gap.

IT'S HARD FOR FOLKS TO TRUST US MORE THAN WE TRUST OURSELVES.

When we fall short, oftentimes we not only lose some trust in ourselves, but also others lose trust in us. It's hard for folks to trust us more than we trust ourselves.

Through coaching many clients through an array of dilemmas where their colleagues and loved ones lost trust in them for one reason or another, these *7 Truths about Trust* emerged and supported them in strengthening the liberatory cultures they were cultivating. As you read through them, highlight any piece of trust you'd like to strengthen for yourself.

NOTES

7 TRUTHS ABOUT TRUST

1. Trust is a verb

Trust is not something you have, it's something you do and build intentionally. Every day we have the choice to either grow our capacity to trust and be trusted, or to undermine it through the actions we take. Be consistent.

2. Trust is a pattern

You don't win someone's trust once and then move on to your other leadership priorities. The evidence of our trustworthiness is our pattern of fulfilled promises, kept commitments, and uncompromised values over time.

3. Trust begets trust

Trust becomes a mark of an organization's culture when the trustor and the trustee are constantly exchanging roles. When you place trust in your team, your team will take that as evidence that they can place their trust in you.

4. Trust invites risk and failure

When leaders trust their teams, they're essentially saying to them: "I believe in you and your potential." Potential is unproven competence and capacity. When you trust in potential, you invite risk, the possibility for failure, innovation, growth, and more trust into your organizational culture. Embrace and transform the "failures" into opportunities for better processes.

5. Trust starts with self

Like with everything in leadership, it all begins with self. The more we trust ourselves, the more we will trust the people we have selected to execute the organizational mission. The more we trust our people, the more we trust their ability to do great work. It is a virtuous cycle that always starts with us.

6. Trust is fragile

It doesn't take much to tear away at trust. Trust is fragile and simple things such as inconsistency or lack of follow-through can undermine it. The accumulation of these small lapses can quickly and quietly add up to distrust and

NOTES

unnecessary assumptions. Sadly, many breaches of trust are predicated on assumptions. To avoid this dynamic, be impeccable with your word and value consistency in your everyday actions.

7. Trust is powerful

There is an ancient proverb that says, "Little drops of water make the mighty ocean." The ocean is powerful. It sustains life, determines global weather patterns, can capsize massive vessels, and can erode coastlines and continents. Such is the case with trust. The simplest and smallest of drops—clarity, consistency, commitment, and character—come together to form an ocean of trust in an organization. When this happens, you and your teams share a powerful bond that can see you through the ebbs and flows of leadership and life.

———————

It's important to emphasize the fragility of trust. So many breaches of trust occur when we don't think to be as detailed, transparent, sensitive, or communicative as we should have been or someone else expected us to be. This dynamic can surface quickly and quietly, making

it important to set conditions to cultivate and rebuild trust by implementing practices like the one below for rebuilding trust. If you don't already have one, consider proactively cocreating a practice for rebuilding trust within your teams based upon the following pillars of rebuilding trust.

PILLARS FOR REBUILDING TRUST

Pillar I: Seek to understand

Before we can take ownership, we have to seek to understand how the breach of trust happened in the first place. This is critical to being able to empathize with the people we let down.

Sometimes we inadvertently break trust by moving too quickly, not considering how our decisions impact others, or by simply not being completely present on any given day. The first step is always to ask the people affected how it happened from their perspective.

NOTES

Pillar II: Take ownership

Once we have a solid understanding of the situation, we have to verbally acknowledge and own the breach. It's important not to make excuses or justify our actions. Instead, we must take responsibility for the outcomes that occurred under our leadership.

Pillar III: Apologize

Apologizing is an emotive action. It cuts through reason and gets to the heart of the matter. While acknowledging a hurt speaks to a person's rational mind, delivering a heartfelt apology speaks to their heart. The key to an authentic apology is to express how the other person's pain is impacting how we see ourselves, our leadership, and the world differently—without centering our own pain. It may feel vulnerable in the moment, and it is one of the most powerful things we can do to rebuild trust with our folks.

Pillar IV: Recommit

The rebuilding process requires new commitments to be made and, most importantly, honored. This is the stage where we think about how to avoid making the same mistake again. It is important to ask those we impacted to tell us what commitments they would like us to make.

With this feedback, we can create a personal growth plan that directly addresses the pain we caused. To stay accountable, great leaders share their plan with those affected and invite ongoing feedback on their efforts.

Pillar V: Give it time

Inquiry, listening, reflection, ownership, action, and time is the rhythm for rebuilding trust. Sometimes we become disheartened when we feel that we have taken all the right steps and things are not yet back to normal. In times like these we must remember that the road back is long and the people who determine its length are those we let down.

———————————•———————————

Now that we've explored both sides of trust and the importance of self-forgiveness, let's dig into the power and importance of forgiving others. I've lost track of how many times I've coached women who bring one dilemma to unpack and their body language reveals that

NOTES

something entirely different needs our focus. Sometimes what is distracting and draining them is a conflict, microaggression, or persistent hurt they haven't released or received reconciliation around. Unresolved conflict and fractured relationships gradually and pervasively zap us of our precious energy and time. Too many of us give our energy away by waiting for others to be ready to reconcile before we do the work of releasing the pain inflicted. Whether the other person is ready to reconcile or not, it's important for us to carve out some peace and resolve for ourselves so that we may free up that time and energy for our renewed purpose.

First, pay attention to your body. Where do you feel the pain or hurt? Consider getting into a comfortable position, closing your eyes, and breathing deeply into the places where you experience the pain. Stay in that position for as long as you're moved and when you're ready, write about what comes up. You may notice that you're grieving and need to create more space to experience your feelings of sadness, anger, or longing. Trust that you'll be guided to the divine right next step for you. For some, that next step may mean engaging with a therapist to explore how the hurt may be connected to childhood trauma and for others it could be writing a letter to the other person involved and burning it as an act of release. And still for others it could be working with a coach or trusted loved one to brainstorm what an authentic conversation with the other person involved could look like.

It's important to acknowledge and embrace the full range of emotions you're feeling—especially anger and sadness. Anger has so much powerful and beautiful data laced within it and is often the catalyst for divine right action. Accept and experience your anger before releasing it through your body in an active way. Too often we suppress it when it's trying to tell us to take a liberated risk. The "Angry Black Woman" trope is just that, a trope created by the sick collective consciousness to protect white fragility. This trope is not our problem.

THIS TROPE IS NOT OUR PROBLEM.

Did you hear me clapping between every word of that last sentence? Just checking. It's just not. Your anger is yours to experience and express in the ways that are authentic to you. Do you remember that feeling you felt when you watched Serena Williams stand up for herself when her character was questioned during that infamous match between her and Naomi Osaka? If not, google it and report back. I felt that experience

NOTES

throughout my body and on so many levels. It was like she was giving me permission to feel and express my justified feelings. What would happen if more of us experienced and expressed our anger at work and in life? Listen, Serena is the GOAT for a reason.

Buried beneath anger is often sadness. Accept that too, because sadness often teaches us about what really matters to us and what unmet needs we need to secure.

- What might you need to ask for?

- What pain needs to be revealed and expressed?

- Who might you need to connect with?

- What hope might you need to release?

Suppressing sadness is an act of self-betrayal and it often ignites myriad health problems including digestive issues, weight gain, chronic stress, and the list goes on and on.

Whatever the path toward forgiveness that you choose, it's important to keep in mind that forgiveness is a gift to yourself in the form of liberated emotions, time, and energy. Forgiveness sets forth an energy of love and renewal that reminds us of one of the redeeming aspects of the human experience. It invites hope and provides an opening for more liberatory relationships. Set an intention for what liberatory relationships look like for you and expect to experience it.

Our lives are a series of peaks and valleys, and it's our work to remain in a constant evolution of rebirthing and resetting ourselves. Gaps are inevitable and necessary. I could have dwelled on L4L hitting a low and wallowed in the painful effects. Instead, I forgave myself, trusted myself, repositioned myself, and came back stronger than ever. It may be time to ask yourself the following questions:

- What ways are you dismissing or overlooking your brilliance?

- What within your sphere may need to be rewritten, updated, or created for the first time?

- What alternative way do you need to look at obstacles or setbacks?

NOTES

- What ways do you need to shift your conditions or environment?

- In what ways have you betrayed yourself and what will set you free?

Choose a question that serves you and see what surfaces.

——————— • NOTES • ———————

Part III

RENEW

P – Protect Your Vibe and Nurture Your Tribe
I – Intentionally Love Yourself
E – Experience Joyfidence

EAT THE PIE; ENJOY LIFE.

ALRIGHT NOW. WE'VE REBIRTHED A NEW WAY OF being, leading, and living, reset our mindsets and conditions, and now it's time to keep that same energy by identifying and incorporating renewal practices that will allow us to enjoy and sustain our level-up. The renewal process is essential for remaining in flow; it's how we thrive while leading boldly. In the section ahead, we'll explore what it means to keep your energy high, your relationships vibrant, and your swag poppin'. As *IndigoWomen*, we're called upon by so many to lead and hold complex conversations, movements, communities, and organizations. We're those "strong friends" who sometimes forget that life is meant to be joy-filled, pleasurable, and free. Some of us don't have an example or blueprint for what that can even look or sound like. Many of our ancestors and elders weren't afforded the opportunity to even dream of a way of being that included so much liberation. Thanks to them, today is a new day. We are their wildest dreams, and we owe it to them to bask in all the joy and abundance they conjured for us. Make one last shift in your seat, refresh that beverage one more time, and intend to further liberate yourself. The statements and questions from clients that inspired this part of the R3 Method™ include the following:

- I don't really know what brings me joy anymore.

- I want to find my voice and feel confident in my leadership style.

- How can I interrupt self-doubt and truly be my biggest cheerleader and believe it?

NOTES

- How can I establish or improve my executive presence when it doesn't mirror white dominant cultural norms?

- How do I tap into and use my intuition when it's not valued at work?

Chapter 7

PROTECT YOUR VIBE AND NURTURE YOUR TRIBE

MANY LEADERS I COACH HAVE A LEADERSHIP style and presence that differs from white dominant cultural norms. They tend to communicate more directly and relationally, inviting a range of reactions from their colleagues and direct reports. While everyone's context is different, the common theme is a desire to lead in ways that feel authentic and are accepted and effective. Many of my clients spend inhumane amounts of cognitive and emotional energy considering and calculating what parts of their intersectional identities to emphasize and deemphasize without betraying and second-guessing themselves. This is energy that could and should be solely channeled into leading effectively. Instead, too many organizations steeped in the sick collective consciousness implicitly and explicitly demand Black women to justify their existence and place within them. In my liberatory culture design work on the L4L side, I notice a promising trend of social impact organizations slowly beginning to own and shift their oppressive conditions that contribute to that shared and pervasive experience.

In our *IndigoWomen* community, we focus on our work of healing. In the renewal process, we deepen our self-awareness about the impact of our emotions on ourselves and others, and identify high-leverage, self-care practices that will continue to rejuvenate us. We begin with two powerful practices:

1. Protect your Vibe.

2. Nurture your Tribe.

Protecting your vibe means integrating self-care practices that will elevate your mood. Meditation, or deep concentrated breathing, calms the mind and nervous system and allows for you to connect with your inner self. This is the most powerful practice for tapping into your intuition and deepening your self-awareness. Other practices that protect your vibe could include setting and honoring boundaries, releasing self-doubt, and celebrating yourself.

Boundaries liberate us. Boundaries aren't exclusionary; they are the anchors that allow us to enjoy life fully and unapologetically. Boundaries help us show up authentically in our relationships and live and lead from a place of strength. Think about and jot down what kind of environment, relationships, and daily flow you need to thrive. Ask yourself what you need to be to give your best. Then, thoughtfully think about how you can communicate your boundaries in a way that invites others to create and communicate boundaries for themselves.

Early in my spiritual growth journey, I attended a spiritual retreat where someone asked me, "What one new habit would dramatically change your life forever and allow you to enjoy your desires?" I took a deep breath and said with clarity, "A daily spiritual practice." Mind you, I didn't have a daily spiritual practice then, nor did I realize it was that important to me until I got asked that question. And I also didn't know that it would require me to set some time and space boundaries in order to honor it.

Instead of focusing on receiving all the answers to my worries and pain points during that retreat, I instead focused on learning more about how to create a daily spiritual practice. Still today, my daily spiritual practice

NOTES

anchors me. It's what protects my vibe and allows me to put challenges and successes in perspective. In our *IndigoWoman Group Coaching Experience* journey, we share and play with various practices throughout the nine-week experience before we invite the woman to map out their daily spiritual practice.

My mornings begin in my meditation room. It's a simple room with my altar, two meditation floor chairs, and altars for each of my two children. My altar has a picture of a few of my ancestors, a container of water, a candle, a bell to wake and ask my ancestors, guides, and angels to act on my behalf, a ring of scriptures, flowers, a few crystals from various points in my life, some spiritual coaching cards, my flute, a fan, sage, and cleansing spray. All of these items fit on a wooden serving tray on top of a small bookcase.

There's not a right or wrong way to build an altar. I've learned through supporting many people in building altars that altars are sacred spaces for connecting with your inner self and only you will know what settles you into this important communion with yourself. You don't need anyone's permission or guidance to create one. You don't need to ascribe to a specific religion or set of beliefs. Several religions support a similar practice.

And you certainly don't need a separate room for it. Before living in my current home, my altar was right next to my bed. What matters is that it invites you to spend quiet, intentional time getting to know and be with yourself. It should feel like a hug rising to hold you. That's it.

IT SHOULD FEEL LIKE A HUG RISING TO HOLD YOU.

Sitting in my floor chair in front of my altar, I ring my bell and pick a scripture. While I was attending a spiritual life-coaching program, someone gifted me a small key ring of forty short scriptures. I use my nondominant hand to select one of those scriptures to set the tone for my day. I read it, consider how it might apply to my life, and set an intention to lean into it when the opportunity comes. I set an intention for the day, close my eyes, and drop into meditation. I usually set a timer for five, ten, or fifteen minutes depending on what I have going on that day or whether my children join me. Afterward, I jot down any fleeting thoughts or whispers of guidance in my journal.

I sometimes get asked whether I pray as well. I experience prayer as a spiritual modality to give praise and thanks, to make requests, and to release heavy burdens. For me, it's most supportive to do this routine at the

NOTES

end of my days. It helps me clear my mind as I prepare to sleep. I have a practice I use called the Letters to Spirit Practice.

LETTERS TO SPIRIT PRACTICE

1. Write a letter to Spirit, or whatever you call your higher power—a stream of consciousness about what you're grateful for, what's worrying you, what you're letting go, and what questions or requests you have.
2. Take a deep breath and set an intention to receive guidance.
3. Write a letter to yourself. Write "Dear (insert your name)" and see what emerges.

I've sorted through many obstacles and stressful situations this way, and so have my clients. Prayer can look like a letter; it can be spoken aloud, and it can be experienced with a partner or loved one to raise the vibration of the energy transmitted. Prayer, and your broader spiritual practice, doesn't have to look a particular way. Free yourself from any limiting associations or connotations to prayer. It's personal time between you and what you call your higher power.

FREE YOURSELF FROM ANY LIMITING ASSOCIATIONS OR CONNOTATIONS TO PRAYER. IT'S PERSONAL TIME BETWEEN YOU AND WHAT YOU CALL YOUR HIGHER POWER.

I use meditation typically in the morning, and often throughout the day, to receive guidance from Spirt. Sometimes I use apps like *Liberate* to guide my meditations, and other times I sit in silence or play a soothing song. I've learned various kinds of meditations and rituals over the years and choose practices that my intuition calls me to use in the moment. I can't express enough that a spiritual practice is personal and needs to only resonate with you. I share parts of mine to ignite ideas for what yours can look like if you don't already have one.

Spiritual practice isn't reserved for just slow or quiet practices. Shonda Rhimes had the main characters in one of her hit TV shows, *Grey's Anatomy*, dance it out when they had particularly stressful days. Dancing is a life-giving spiritual practice. I love to dance, twerk, and sing made-up songs throughout the day. Each time I do it, I'm connecting with my inner self and emanating joy. Speaking of Shonda, if you haven't read her book, *Year of*

NOTES

Yes, add it to your queue. Saying yes is a spiritual practice. Anytime we connect with and honor our True selves, we are exercising a spiritual practice.

As beings who are a part of at least two marginalized groups, it's important for us to be mindful of the environments we live, work, and play within. Many of the workplace environments that we work within weren't designed for us to belong—let alone thrive within. Systemic racism and gender-based bias swirl in and out of workplace meetings, practices, structures, and policies creating trauma-inducing experiences for far too many of us. Many organizations, especially post global racial uprising, attempt to address this long-standing crisis by providing support to those marginalized, while ignoring the conditions within said organizations that create the trauma that those marginalized experience. The *Harvard Business Review* recently published a piece highlighting the damaging effects of labeling women and women of color as having imposter syndrome, positioning them as having the problem that needs to be addressed rather than the workplace cultures that desperately need redesigning.[10]

---

10. Tulshyan, Ruchika and Jodi-Ann Burey, "End Imposter Syndrome in Your Workplace," *Harvard Business Review*, 14 July 2021, https://hbr.org/2021/07/end-imposter-syndrome-in-your-workplace.

Clients often contemplate what workplace boundaries they need in order to thrive. They've felt, and at times succumbed to, the pressures to assimilate to white dominant culture norms—predicated on the sick collective consciousness—in order to keep their jobs, maintain political and social capital, rise within their organizations, and position themselves for future career opportunities. They reflect upon times they centered white comfort by not giving feedback to white people in decision-making roles, saying very little in various meetings, not interrupting or speaking up about various microaggressions and workplace biases, or not offering diverse perspectives about an organization's strategic direction. We're all taught both explicitly and implicitly to prioritize white comfort in order to appear less threatening. Meanwhile, this forced self-betrayal often manifests as exhaustion, self-doubt, depression, poor health, isolation, and disillusionment. Within the *IndigoWoman Group Coaching Experience*, we explore their financial and workplace condition needs through the lens of their JCC—what they are uniquely positioned to do and the kind of lifestyle that they desire. Our ancestors didn't make endless and unconscionable sacrifices in order for

NOTES

us to settle for what's offered or currently exists. Never confuse what's offered with what you're worth.

Our ancestors want us to thrive, to live the lives they could only dream about. Picking up where they left off is going to require us to tell the truth about what truly matters to us, how toxic workplace cultures have set conditions that invite us to betray ourselves and others, and what risks we're willing to take. Accepting these truths sometimes looks like advocating for policy and systemic changes that dismantle white supremacy culture characteristics and reconstruct liberatory workplace culture characteristics; sometimes it looks like attaining board leadership positions to hold organizations accountable to said changes; and other times it looks like developing a succession or exit plan in order to find or create an environment that has conditions in place for us to be able to thrive. There are multiple paths to take based upon one's unique context. Regardless of the chosen path, it's critical that we have a self-care rhythm that supports us being self-compassionate, authentic, grounded, and free. In what way will you commit to protecting your vibe?

NEVER CONFUSE WHAT'S OFFERED WITH WHAT YOU'RE WORTH.

Existing within the sick collective consciousness while raising your own consciousness also requires consistent fellowship with a life-giving, supportive Tribe of people who see, hear, know, honor, and uplift you. Navigating the sick collective consciousness is an uphill battle riddled with constant gaslighting and varied, inconsistent spurts of progress, leaving us prone to second-guess and shrink ourselves in subversive ways. We must surround ourselves with people with shared experiences who can be our mirrors, understand our challenging circumstances, and call us into a higher expression of who we are. No one can do that for us like we can.

IN WHAT WAY WILL YOU COMMIT TO PROTECTING YOUR VIBE?

WE MUST SURROUND OURSELVES WITH PEOPLE WITH SHARED EXPERIENCES WHO CAN BE OUR MIRRORS, UNDERSTAND OUR CHALLENGING CIRCUMSTANCES, AND CALL US INTO A HIGHER EXPRESSION OF WHO WE ARE.

Nurturing Your Tribe means being deliberate about who you form deep relationships with, and how you show up for each person or group in your life. It's important to be fully present with them, accept them for who they are, be open to receiving their language of

NOTES

love, and carve out time to play with them. I've spoken a few times about the influence the people in our lives have on our social awareness. Our capacity to have empathy for others directly affects the depth of our Tribes. Let's break that down.

Tribe can have different meanings for different people. When I use this word, I mean those people who are kindred spirits and those you trust. These are people who will tell you the truth, expect you to tell the truth, and will call you higher. These are people who want to see you win, will celebrate with you when you do, and will support you when you fall. Folk in your Tribe remind you of your magnificence when you forget, call you in when you step out of alignment, and make time to be present with you. Leadership can be very lonely, and it's crucial that we have a Tribe we can lean on.

Self-care is also about prioritizing our relationships with loved ones. As communal beings, we have natural needs to connect. When I work with leaders on the brink of or in complete burnout, a common thread is they've de-prioritized the important relationships within their lives. They've gone weeks, months, or even years without talking to and being with people who fill their cups and remind them of what really matters in life. Some of them may be physically present with loved ones but aren't emotionally present.

An executive client recently said, "I'm almost fifty, and I'm embarrassed to say that I don't have a Tribe and am not quite sure how to create one." This client is far from alone. I hear this sentiment a lot. Many of us are the first, or among the first, in our families to graduate from college and have careers that afford us to live somewhat comfortably. This transition often required a laser focus on succeeding in higher education and within the workplace. Many of us financially support other family members and have children and partners to nurture and support. I invite clients to examine what it looks like for them to nurture various people within their lives. Oftentimes, the nurturing looks like doing what others request of them without an examination of what they actually have to give. It looks like taking on disproportionately more tasks at work than colleagues at the same level. It looks like loaning money to various family members without agreed upon pay schedules. It looks like not setting boundaries and clear expectations for adult children living at home who are transitioning to the workforce. These and many other examples are manifestations of not putting ourselves first. This is why Protect Your

NOTES

Vibe comes before Nurture Your Tribe. Many times, we don't yet have the boundaries in place to be able to attend to other life-giving relationships.

When focusing on cultivating a Tribe, I guide clients to make small, immediate commitments that allow them to spend time with high-vibrating people who would appreciate an authentic relationship. One small commitment toward that end could be calling an old friend you haven't spoken to in a long time. It could also mean reaching out to a kindred spirit in one of the groups or memberships you're already a part of. It could mean posting about an interest on social media and reaching out to those who share that interest to connect in real time. It's important to note that I said "high-vibrating." When I say that, I mean people who value growth, learning, connection, love, and reciprocity. These are people who avoid gossip and instead prefer to talk about how they can be and give their best in various aspects of their lives. They have abundant mindsets and want everyone in their sphere to win. They often congratulate or uplift others and share both their challenges and knowledge that they gain along the way.

Tribes can be as small as two or three people or as extensive as a group of twenty women like in our

IndigoWoman Group Coaching Experience. Each person in your Tribe may or may not know each other. What's important is that you create time and space for each person. Tribes differ from Support Teams; Support Teams are those professional practitioners who support your mind, body, and soul in specific and often contractual ways. These people can include therapists, spiritual teachers or guides, coaches, mentors, healers, or personal trainers. Support teams are incredibly important and should shift as your life shifts. The support within Support Teams is one way and extremely beneficial, whereas the support within Tribes is reciprocal and provides an outlet for play, lightness, and joy.

When was the last time you played? Do you even know what that means for you? I didn't until a few years ago when I focused on play for a whole year. Many of us are over-responsible and under-playful. Yes, I did just make up those words! And it's true. We are here to thrive and part of thriving is having shoulder-pumping fun. Our Tribes should be those people who see all of us—not just what we can provide for them. We need

MANY OF US ARE OVER-RESPONSIBLE AND UNDER-PLAYFUL.

NOTES

places where we can just *be,* and our Tribes are great places to do just that.

In what way will you commit to nurturing your Tribe and Support Team?

Chapter 8

INTENTIONALLY LOVE YOURSELF

THE VERY ACT OF REBIRTHING, RESETTING, AND renewing yourself is a radical act of self-love. Self-love is an acceptance and appreciation of who we are, an act of kindness and self-compassion, and a nurturing of our growth and wellbeing.

Virtually everything we've explored together is undergirded by a love and reverence for self. Desiring and committing to be the best version of yourself demonstrates a recognition that you are a gift to this world. This is an incredible feat when we live in a society that constantly sanctions hate, indifference, fetishization, disdain, appropriation, disregard, and even death thrown our way. And here we are, loving ourselves unapologetically. We're declaring that we are worthy and deserving of the very best in life. Abundance

SELF-LOVE IS AN ACCEPTANCE AND APPRECIATION OF WHO WE ARE, AN ACT OF KINDNESS AND SELF-COMPASSION, AND A NURTURING OF OUR GROWTH AND WELLBEING.

is our birthright. I am bowing the deepest of bows. Take a breath.

TAKE A BREATH. Our mere existence is miraculous and, when you add our audacity to be free, joyous, brilliant, beautiful, and versatile, it can seem like we're too much. I hear this sentiment echoed by a lot of my clients and I want to remind us that us being too much for anyone is *not* our issue. The only thing there is for you to do is to keep caring for and loving you. Do you hear folk complaining about the sun being too bright? Nah. They put on some sunglasses and keep it moving. Folk will either rise to meet your light or they will adjust.

THEY PUT ON SOME SUNGLASSES AND KEEP IT MOVING. FOLK WILL EITHER RISE TO MEET YOUR LIGHT OR THEY WILL ADJUST.

For many of my clients, it was when they didn't fully accept and embrace the fullness of themselves when they experienced the most anxiety and feelings of being overwhelmed. Clients have described instances when they shrank or hid themselves by taking positions they were too big for, dating people who weren't worthy of them, and not throwing their hat into the ring for positions they convinced themselves they weren't "ready" for. If I'm stepping on your toes, the first

---

NOTES

step is to intentionally love yourself in the ways that feel authentic to you. When we intentionally love ourselves, we unlock more information about what we need and desire. Consider the various ways to actively love yourself below and highlight what might bring more self-compassion your way:

ACTIVELY LOVE YOURSELF

- Affirming your dopeness
- Saying positive things to yourself
- Saying no
- Saying yes
- Forgiving yourself when you fall short
- Meeting your own needs
- Being assertive
- Prioritizing your health and wellbeing
- Not letting others take advantage of or abuse you
- Spending time around people who support you and build you up (and avoiding people who don't)
- Asking for help
- Letting go of grudges or anger that holds you back
- Advocating for yourself

- Experiencing and valuing your feelings

- Making healthy choices most of the time

- Choosing roles that amplify your strengths

- Leading and living in alignment with your values

- Pursuing your interests and goals

- Resting

- Challenging yourself

- Holding yourself accountable

- Eating healthy, high-vibration foods

- Celebrating yourself

- Accepting your imperfections

- Decluttering and decorating your space

- Setting realistic expectations

- Listing your 3 big wins at the end of each day

- Buying yourself flowers

- Noticing your progress and effort

- Taking a nap

We talked about the importance of self-compassion when we rebirthed and I'm going to spiral back to it here because it is truly revolutionary for us. Many of us have been either directly or indirectly taught to "suck it up and

NOTES

keep it moving" and it pains me to think of how this has eroded our love and regard for ourselves. It's critical that we validate our feelings, experiences, and needs; otherwise, we become susceptible to sabotaging ourselves by treating others with the same disregard. The next time you feel overwhelmed or triggered in any way, pause and literally name the feelings that emerge for you by completing this prompt: "This is a tough moment. I'm feeling . . . "

"THIS IS A TOUGH MOMENT. I'M FEELING . . . "

Just the act of naming what you're feeling can release tension and provide a clue for what you might need.

When my clients reach various milestones, I often ask them how they celebrated themselves and I'm often met with either silence or a, "Ha! What's that?!" Celebrating ourselves is like self-compassion on steroids—and it's a must. We know how to celebrate and uplift each other. There's nothing quite like that feeling of another Sista looking you up and down with a smile and saying, "You did that!" We know how to amplify each other like no one else and we must get comfortable, if we aren't already, with amplifying and celebrating our own milestones. It's important to expand what celebrating yourself can look like. It can look like calling someone within your Tribe to share the good news. It could look like pausing what you're working on to blast and dance to your favorite song. It could look like purchasing something that makes you feel beautiful. It could also look like treating yourself to a favorite meal or new body practice like acupuncture or massage. Whatever mode of celebration you choose, please make sure that it brings you joy and allows you to fully focus on acknowledging your brilliance and beauty.

Here's the thing, self-love is contagious, inspiring, and powerful. It's both a gift to yourself and others. It's hard to be something you can't see. In a recent *IndigoWoman Group Coaching Experience* session, a woman mentioned that she'd never seen a Black woman who centered self-care. Others cosigned and then another woman challenged the group to spend the next week intentionally looking for examples. A week later, one woman mentioned memories of her mother shifting jobs to have more time for her children and herself. Another woman mentioned remembering clear boundaries that a former Black manager set around work hours. We talked about how we likely don't notice all of the examples because prioritizing ourselves has yet to become normalized for us.

NOTES

I challenge all of us to be more vocal and public about how we're prioritizing ourselves. Too many of us are waiting for permission to put ourselves first. What would happen if we all prioritized ourselves and celebrated it? How might it impact our health, families, and organizations? What would we create? Who would we be? Let's find out.

I CHALLENGE ALL OF US TO BE MORE VOCAL AND PUBLIC ABOUT HOW WE'RE PRIORITIZING OURSELVES.

Intentionally loving ourselves looks like nurturing our growth and wellbeing—exactly what we're doing in partnership right now. This can also look like hiring a coach or taking a radical self-care trip where you travel alone for the sole purpose of reconnecting with yourself. It could be advocating for a sabbatical at work or a job-embedded task that stretches you in some way. And it can look like doing absolutely nothing. Yes, nothing. Rest is revolutionary. If you're not already familiar with her, I highly recommend listening to podcast interviews by Tricia Hersey, founder of The Nap Ministry. Her work is game changing and will invite future generations to dream a grander vision of liberation than we can conceive right now.

Finally, and perhaps most importantly, intentionally loving ourselves is deciding to experience joy. Cultivating joy begins with cultivating an awareness of, a reverence and love for, our bodies. Body awareness is the ability to recognize where our body is in space or a period of time. Our muscles and joints send our brain information about our body and how it moves. Body awareness helps us understand how to relate to objects and people in the literal sense, as in how far to bend our knees or back to pick up an object, and in the spiritual sense, as in whether someone poses a threat. Body awareness is about the mind, body, spirit connection and how we're accessing the information in all three places. Many of us have heard the saying "The body never lies." And many of us have experienced those moments when our bodies begin to sweat or our breath becomes shallow before we're aware that we're experiencing anxiety. My body tends to pick up weight and hold fat I would otherwise burn when I'm in toxic relationships. What I carry emotionally tends to show up physically as well. When I released those toxic relationships, my cortisol levels would decrease and my metabolism would increase resulting in weight loss. I didn't become aware of that experience until it happened about three times

NOTES

and I got still enough to notice the pattern. It's important to turn whatever judgments we have about how our body looks, functions, or feels into curiosities. Ask yourself what your body needs and desires.

- What is your body trying to tell you about how and with whom you spend your time?

- When does your body thrive?

Answers to these questions could invite you to reposition yourself in powerful ways.

When talking about the significance of our bodies, a friend of mine said, "Our bodies are the conduits through which we experience our environment. Our experiences are only as healthy as our vehicles." We aren't able to accomplish anything without our bodies. Aside from washing and moving your body, what have you done to express a deep reverence or gratitude for it?

OUR BODIES ARE EXTRAORDINARY.

Our bodies are extraordinary. They multitask like I've never seen—ensure we're breathing, wake the next day, recover from viruses and bacteria, create life, produce nutrients for babies, and so much more. When was the last time you celebrated what your body has, is, and will do for you? Some of my clients decide to be more intentional about dressing and adorning their bodies to express reverence. Some got tattoos or drastic new hairstyles while others invested in some body jewelry that brought them joy. We have one shot in this body in this lifetime. In what ways will you honor and celebrate your body?

WE HAVE ONE SHOT IN THIS BODY IN THIS LIFETIME. IN WHAT WAYS WILL YOU HONOR AND CELEBRATE YOUR BODY?

On a deeper level, what I've come to personally understand and experience is that whenever I decide to level-up in leadership and life, I need to begin with leveling up with my body in some way. Over the years, that has looked like partnering with a nutritionist to learn more about the specific foods that my body craves, partnering with a personal trainer, doing quarterly fruit and vegetable cleanses to detoxify my body from food toxins, and most recently joining the Peloton community. Each time and with each path, the purpose was to get physically stronger as a signal to my mind and spirit to strengthen and elevate as well.

NOTES

Something I often say is, "You can fake confidence, but you can't fake joy." Although we can achieve confidence when we have external success, we can thus compartmentalize it to certain areas of our lives. For example, we may feel confident at work, and yet be full of self-doubt in our personal or romantic lives. When women in our *IndigoWomen* community set a goal related to confidence, we begin with a decision to choose joy.

Joy is an enduring, long-lasting, and powerful feeling of inner peace, contentment, and completion. When in this state, we can innovate, relate, and lead from our best selves. Rooting ourselves in joy keeps us rooted in our authenticity without the need to look for external motivation or validation. In the *IndigoWomen* community we call this shift in mindset going "from confidence to joyfidence." Joyfidence is a full-body, holistic experience achieved through deepened self-awareness and life-giving relationships. Thriving isn't about having fleeting moments of happiness or success; it's about emanating a

JOY IS AN ENDURING, LONG-LASTING, AND POWERFUL FEELING OF INNER PEACE, CONTENTMENT, AND COMPLETION. WHEN IN THIS STATE, WE CAN INNOVATE, RELATE, AND LEAD FROM OUR BEST SELVES.

radiant energy that invites others to raise their own frequencies. Joy is contagious, it's resistance against the sick collective consciousness, and it allows us to live and lead with conviction, ease, and grace. Count it all joy, Sis.

NOTES

NOTES

Before I Let Go . . .

LIKE IN ANY COACHING ENGAGEMENT, I END WITH an invitation to reflect and commit.

REFLECT

- What will it mean for you, those you lead, and those you love to rebirth, reset, and renew?

- What and who will you call upon for support along the way?

COMMIT

Set an intention for how you'd like to experience your leadership and life. Feel free to use this prompt:

- My intention is to . . . (experience) for the purpose of . . . (desired outcome).

EXPECT
TO
THRIVE.

In love and liberation,
Shayna Renee

NOTES

Acknowledgments

I'D LIKE TO THANK SPIRIT, MY ANCESTORS, GUIDES, and angels, known and unknown, for supporting me in birthing this book. I deeply appreciate my shaman, Richael Faithful, for reminding me that "we teach what we need to learn" as I flowed through the uncertainty embedded within the book writing process. And for those times that I forgot Richael's wise words, I deeply appreciate members of my Tribe, my inner circle, for reminding me who I am, what I'm called to do, and that I'll always have a soft place to land.

I cannot thank Cohorts 1, 2, 3, 4, 5, and 6 of the *IndigoWomen* community enough for their divine yes, trust in themselves, the process, each other, and me. Their stories, journeys, experiences, challenges, and successes brought the R3 Method to life in ways I couldn't have imagined. The cohorts quite literally wouldn't have run without our partners, supporters, and the Vibe Tribe—Sophia Scott and Hannah Coleman. Thank you for gracefully honoring our values in your unique ways and for embodying our vision and mission.

Acknowledgments

And then there are my two greatest sources of inspiration, my children—Judah and Joelle. Thank you for
believing in me, being who you each are, and for thoughtfully choosing the book cover. You did that! :)

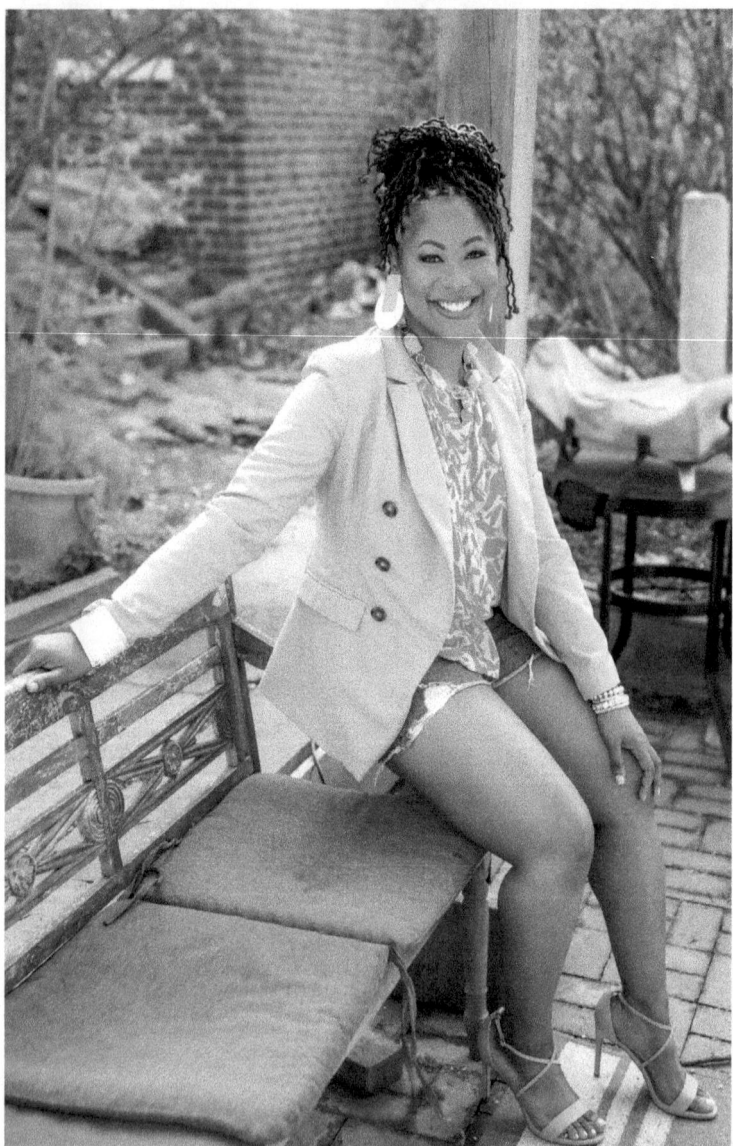

About the Author

SHAYNA RENEE HAMMOND IS A LEADERSHIP AND life coach who has developed thousands of leaders within the education and nonprofit sectors for nearly twenty years. She is the founder and CEO of Lead For Liberation, a leadership-development organization dedicated to guiding organizations, school districts, teams, and communities to demystify and operationalize liberatory cultures. Through Lead For Liberation's support, schools and organizations across America have experienced unprecedented school growth and achievement outcomes; inclusive school and organizational cultures; and strengthened teacher, principal, and executive leader effectiveness and retention.

Inspired by the success of Lead For Liberation in the education and nonprofit sectors and her calling to raise global consciousness, Shayna recently founded IndigoWomen, a coaching practice dedicated to creating spaces, methods, and conditions for Black women in leadership to thrive. In this capacity, Shayna coaches Black women executive leaders and entrepreneurs from around the globe in a spiritually inspired and research-based coaching methodology created by and for Black women. IndigoWomen's methodologies and spaces inspire and equip Black women in leadership to rejuvenate their minds, bodies, and spirits so that they can lead more authentically, effectively, and sustainably.

Shayna extends the love and power she brings to her work beyond her role as an entrepreneur by serving as a spiritual life coach and facilitator for Harriet's Apothecary—a healer's collective led by Black cis women, queer, and trans healers in partnership with ancestors and the earth itself. She also serves as a board trustee for a few organizations including Livelihood Trust, a community economic development organization, and St. Patrick's Episcopal Day School in Washington, DC.

Prior to founding Lead For Liberation and IndigoWomen, Shayna led the national development of teacher leaders at KIPP Foundation; supported principals within the Baltimore City School System; led the highest-performing middle school in Baltimore, Maryland; and was an award-winning teacher.

Shayna earned a bachelor's degree in kinesiology with minors in business and English from James Madison University, a master's degree in the art of teaching from Johns Hopkins University, and a master's of education degree focusing on administration and supervision from National-Louis University. She completed the Certificate in Leadership Coaching Program at Georgetown University and is also a part-time faculty member at the University of Pennsylvania Graduate School of Education's PENN Literacy Network.

When Shayna isn't coaching, facilitating, or leading, she's enjoying quality time with her two children, Judah and Joelle; learning a new sport; showing up for her Tribe; or exploring a new venue for spiritual growth and renewal.

I would appreciate your feedback on what chapters helped you most and what you would like to see in future books.

If you enjoyed this book and found it helpful, please leave a REVIEW on Amazon.

Visit me or join the IndigoWomen community at

WWW.INDIGOWOMENCOMMUNITY.COM

THANK YOU!

www.ingramcontent.com/pod-product-compliance
Lightning Source LLC
Chambersburg PA
CBHW062218080426
42734CB00010B/1937